DISCOVER
YOUR PAST LIVES

DISCOVER
YOUR PAST LIVES

Brad and Francie Steiger

Whitford Press

1469 Morstein Road
West Chester, Pennsylvania 19380 USA

International Standard Book Number: 0-914918-76-1
Library of Congress Catalog Card Number: 87-62094

Published by Whitford Press
Distributed by Schiffer Publishing Ltd.
1469 Morstein Road
West Chester, Pennsylvania 19380

Manufactured in the United States of America

This book may be purchased from the publisher.
Please include $2.00 postage
Try your bookstore first.

Table of Contents

1

How to Use This Book

Let us begin by answering that obvious question that some of you will want to ask: "Why should I discover my past lives? What can I possibly gain from knowing anything about prior existences? I'm having a hard enough time with this lifetime!"

Well, first of all, we look upon knowledge of past lives as a form of awareness that can help everyone to get it together in the present-life experience, which in turn will help shape a more positive, productive, peaceful future.

Whether past-life recall is pure fantasy or the actual memory of a prior existence, we have observed many men and women who have obtained definite and profound release from a present pain or phobia by reliving the origin of the problem in some real or alleged former existence.

When a person relives what may be a past life, he or she becomes capable of accepting responsibility for a past action that may have been performed in another lifetime. Once the subject has made the transfer of responsibility to the present life and has recognized that the "fault" lies in a time far removed from current concerns, he or she is able to deal with the matter without embarrassment or shame.

Such extended awareness can bring you much more than past-life memories, and even more than the resolution of specific current problems. By exploring prior-life experiences, you may truly come to "know thyself" and to recall physical and mental skills you have mastered in other lifetimes. You may rediscover talents that will bring greater creativity to your present-life experience. You may relearn how to become more efficient in the performance of daily tasks. By exploring past lives and by expanding your awareness, you have nothing to lose and everything to gain.

Increasing one's awareness has such wonderful by-products. All the pleasures that you derive through your senses will be enhanced. Your sight, your hearing, your touch, your smell, your taste will all become keener. You will be capable of detecting subtleties that you've never noticed before. You will achieve a deeper insight into the actions of others and therefore will gain greater control of your life and yourself.

With such self-mastery you will begin to notice an increase in your extrasensory ability, your ESP. An enrichment of these abilities will enable you to transform your entire life into one that is fulfilling, pleasurable, and happy.

Really basic to the therapeutic benefits of past-life recall is the medically attested fact that the physical body conducts itself according to the beliefs of the mind. Psychologists have long realized that discovering the cause of an existing condition releases the *effect* of its hold on the patient. Medical doctors know that diseases have emotional as well as physical origins. A belief in the theory of reincarnation is *not* necessary for the subject to experience a benefit from the cathartic visions that s/he receives while reliving a past lifetime. Nor are we interested in *proving* the reality of reincarnation to anyone. Our only intention is to help as many people as we possibly can to put their lives together in more productive ways.

However, to keep the record straight, *we accept a theory of rebirth as integral to our own reality construct.* Later in this book we will explain our hypothesis of reincarnation as well as alternative theories on the subject.

For now, suffice it to say that we have come more and more to believe that each of us has the ability to get in touch with some aspect of our past—our own or that which exists in the common, collective unconcious—and that this ability can be extremely useful to us if we are troubled with deep problems and phobias, or if we simply want to become more aware of who we really are.

Yes, we believe that the past—or an idea of the past— can become a very useful tool that we can utilize to our great benefit.

Let's run that by one more time.

That's right. We said an "idea of the past." Although we are all aware that there has been an actual, historical, material past for us and for the world, at the same time we must admit that the Past—with a capital "P"—is now little more than an idea, no more real than fantasy.

Remember that challenge from Philosophy 101: "Prove that the entire world, complete with all the old ruins, all the ancient artifacts, and all collective and individual memories, was not just created three seconds ago."

Sure, we chuckle at such intriguing conundrums. Someone will always get a little agitated, though, and state that he *knows* the past exists because he has a head full of precise memories of his past.

The thing is, regardless of how exact your personal memories may be, you must admit that what you are really carrying around inside your head are the *images* of birthday parties or troop trains or weddings or funerals or stock car races or Times Square on New Year's Eve or whatever, not the *actual* things and events themselves.

And sometimes a person with the keenest of memories has discovered to his possible irritation or embarrassment that if there were other witnesses to an event of which he may have been boasting, those witnesses might accuse him of having added a great deal of fantasy to his memory.

Certain therapists have suggested that nearly all acts of memory are little more than impractical fantasy activity. They wonder how much it profits a man or a woman to revel in sentimental replays of first kisses, first days of school, and last days of summer romances past. They can see no useful function in worrying about past occasions that one wishes had happened differently.

Our contention is that *memories* of the past, *images* of the past, *ideas* of the past—real or fantasized—can be used to build a more complete and fully-realized life in the here and now. We believe in putting the past to work in order to construct a brighter, more fulfilling future.

And we believe that this book can offer you both a better today and a more dynamic tomorrow by teaching you how to use your memories of actual or possible past lives as tools of awareness and expanded consciousness.

Now that we have answered—more or less successfully, we hope—the question of what you can gain from knowledge of your past lives, we must face the second-most-obvious question: "How can a *book* help me to discover my own past-life memories?"

In our awareness seminars we induce an altered state of consciousness in each of the participants; we guide them through a series of inner journeys that enable them to view important past lives, to receive vision teachings, and to obtain glimpses of future lives. In this state of extended awareness each participant is able to meet his or her Karmic Counterpart, that particular past life that is most responsible for what has occurred to him or her in the present-life experience. We especially strive to permit each seminar participant to receive a more complete understanding of what his or her true mission on Earth is to be.

Men and women emerge from the seminar experience

with a much clearer total picture of why they came together with the family, friends, lovers, mates, and associates of their present-life experiences. They have also been shown that they have within them a multidimensional faculty, a spiritual essence, that interacts with energies that permeate all life on this planet—and perhaps all life in the universe.

If you use this book correctly, you will be able to experience all the inner journeys and extended awarenesses of our seminar participants. There is no question that you can obtain excellent results if you choose to use this book to explore your past lives and foster your own inner growth. You will find this book especially effective if, sooner or later, you *share* the exercises and techniques with another person. Some of you may even want to assemble small groups for insightful collective experiences.

We have included in this book a number procedures that will place you in an extremely relaxed consciousness state so that the questions you read later on will provoke meaningful images that you can jot down for later study.

For superior results from any of the techniques we have shared with you in this book, record the relaxation techniques and the exerices on tape in your own voice, then play the tape back so that you can serve as your own guide. Don't give any credence to that old fear about going into a hypnotic trance and sleeping on and on like Rip Van Winkle. If you should fall into an altered state while listening to your previously recorded techniques, you will simply awaken within a brief time, just as you would from any normal sleep.

You will also find that our techniques will be most effective for you if you select a time of day when you know you will not be disturbed. Find a place where you will not be bothered by anyone, so that you may lie down or sit comfortably or assume a yoga or meditative position.

If you read the relaxation procedures aloud to a friend, spouse, or family member, you may find that you have brought about an altered state of consciousness in that individual. At this point it is very important that you not experiment on your own by asking any fanciful or bizarre questions. Follow our procedures exactly and you will enjoy excellent results with no possibility of problems.

Until you become adept at altered states techniques do not be afraid to use your imagination to "prime the pump" a bit. Many of you remember or have heard about how people used to have to pour a dipper of water down the top of an old pump before anyone could get it to bring up fresh water. Your imagination can serve as that initial dipper of "priming water."

If, for example, it is suggested that you conjure up a castle or a temple in your mind, you may not instantly receive a clear, independent visualization. But you know, surely, what a castle or a temple might look like, so go ahead and imagine one from your own memory. It may be a temple or a castle that you have actually seen and visited...or one that you may have seen only in a book or a motion picture, but whatever it is, it will work for you.

Once you have your imagined castle or temple firmly fixed in your mind's eye, you will be amazed how quickly some other castle or temple will come springing to life and take complete charge of your thoughts.

The important thing is that you not block our suggestions or permit your conscious mind to interfere with your creative levels of awareness. Do not waste even a second worrying about what kind of image you should see.

So whatever we suggest in these exercises, do not hesitate to use your own imagination if the image does not appear at once. In each instance the important thing is that you respond to our suggestions and that you do not block the flow of energy from us to you.

Yes, even though this is an assortment of ink and paper in your hands, a product of printing technology, our energy is still being transmitted to you. And while you are playing "Let's Pretend" with us, the images that you are supposed to see for your greater development will appear.

Even now as we write this book, we are transmitting a vibration of unconditional love to you who will one day read these words. We will not argue with you. We will not attack you. We will not insult your belief construct. By the same token, neither do we wish to be insulted or attacked. Relax and give yourself a chance to receive our message.

Know as you experience these pages with us that we are living our belief construct. We truly believe in the reality of past lives and the ability inherent in humankind to rise to higher dimensions of awareness. We seek in these pages to do our utmost to aid you in achieving a greater understanding of yourself, but if you are to understand us you must bear in mind that we totally believe in what we are doing and what we are saying.

If you sincerely desire to permit your awareness to grow during the reading of these techniques, you will have a wonderful sense of joy as you receive guidance for your inner voyage of self-discovery. But always keep in mind that although we strive to be as helpful as we can in providing you with the tools you may use in your independent quest, we cannot walk your path of life for you. We consider ourselves to be light bearers, and we wish only to shine a light so that you may see your own path more clearly.

During the past several years we have worked with men and women from an astonishingly wide variety of religious, philosophical, and spiritual belief constructs. We have never found anyone who felt that our technique could not be compatible with his or her personal path of enlightenment.

We have written this book so that we might share with you an attitude of unconditional love and a sincere desire to aid you in achieving a higher state of awareness. If you truly wish it, you will be able to undergo a series of experiences that will help you to make more complete sense out of your life than ever before.

And now, before you begin your first exercise, I, Brad,

remind you to..."Remain steadfast to your quest, and walk always, in balance."

And I, Francie, add..."Heaven be with you!"

2

Awareness Warm-Up Exercises

Before we take you on any deep spiritual explorations within your psyche, we'd first like to guide you in some awareness-stretching exercises.

It is the wise athlete who always warms up his or her muscles before engaging in any new or strenuous physical activity. So it is that the wise seeker of spiritual truths will endeavor to expand his or her consciousness as much as possible before exploring any new understandings or revelatory insights.

The following awareness warm-up exercises will prove extremely valuable to any reader who comes to the area of past-life exploration as a complete novice. At the same time we feel that even the more experienced seeker will find these techniques both provocative and stimulating, making him or her more receptive.

Where Do Your Thoughts Flow? Assume a comfortable position sitting or lying down. Take a few deep breaths, inhaling and exhaling slowly but comfortably.

Now that you have stilled your mental and physical processes, become aware of where your thoughts flow. What precisely are you aware of?

Is it the clock ticking on the wall? The sound of the neighbors in the next apartment? Is it some part of your own body?

Once you have isolated *where* your awareness has gone, ask yourself *why*.

What is there about the clock that pulled your awareness to it? Was it the sound of the ticking? Or is there something about time and its ebb and flow that captures your attention?

Whatever ensnares your awareness, enter into that person, object, or emotion and focus on *why*, in the stillness of your mental and physical processes, you were pulled to it.

When you have isolated your thoughts about the object and the reasons that your awareness has flowed to it, permit yourself to fantasize. See yourself in another situation with, again, for example, a clock.

Was there a crisis situation in which you were penalized for being late? Was there a most important time when you were watching the clock? Was there a moment of confrontation when time ran out for you?

Whatever the object, let yourself go with a portrayal of your being involved with it in another life experience.

What and Who Don't You Think About? After you have quieted yourself and assumed a comfortable position that you can maintain for quite some time, permit your mind to focus on a number of situations, people, places, objects.

After you have done this for a few minutes, suddenly ask yourself: "*What* am I *not* thinking about? *Who* am I *not* thinking about?"

See what comes into your awareness. You may pick up on a person or a situation from your present life, and you will have gained from the confrontation. But you may begin to have images come to mind that you will identify as having originated in a previous-life experience. Whatever the case, stay with the thoughts and images and see what discoveries you are able to make.

If you are unable to gain the flow of a scene in which you

are doing something unpleasant, interject into your memory the words: "I am still avoiding thinking about _____!"

Complete the statement with whatever comes into your mind, regardless of how ridiculous it might at first seem to be.

Don't censor the thoughts in any way.

Whatever has come to you may provide you with valuable insights about certain kinds of life experiences that you have been avoiding. More important, perhaps, are the insights you will gain as to why you have not wished to confront certain situations.

Let us say that the matter you are avoiding turns out to be a particular person. If this is a person whom you know from your present-life experience, focus on that individual and ask yourself why you avoid interacting with him or her.

Is there something about this person's face, body structure, mannerisms, attitudes?

Has this person done something specific to you that has caused you to avoid additional experiences with him or her?

If you cannot put your finger on why you have avoided this person in your present-life experiences, fantasize about him or her in a past-life situation. Say to yourself: "I see _____ and we are about to _____."

Complete the sentence with whatever comes to mind. Again, do nothing to censor the thoughts. Permit them total escape from the unconscious levels of your mind.

As the images come, stay with them, examine them for discoveries about how you can deal with the person whom you have been avoiding.

Establish an insight from this past-life linkup as to why you have come together in your present-life experiences.

Are you to complete a lesson left unlearned, to finish a task undone?

Have you been avoiding this person so that you might avoid completing the karmic payoff that would reestablish balance in your life?

Body Scan: This exercise is performed best while lying in a comfortable position. Quiet yourself and go inward. Close your eyes and shut yourself off visually from your surroundings. Permit your body to become as comfortable as possible.

Relax and begin to focus on your breathing. Imagine that there is a cloud of pure oxygen before your nose. Let the cloud be your favorite color.

Now, as you breath, visualize that cloud of pure oxygen moving down into your lungs. See it expanding your chest; see it inflating the air sacs in your lungs. See it carrying off any particles of impurities which may be there.

Now exhale and see it making a circle in your lungs before it moves back up through your throat and out your nostrils. Continue this breathing exercise until you visualize that the air being exhaled has become as clean and as pure as the colored oxygen being inhaled.

Now imagine your brain beginning to scan your body, probing every limb, every section, until you begin to focus on one particular body part.

What sensations are you feeling from that body part?

What makes it feel more distinct than your other body parts?

Is it more uncomfortable?

Why is it continuing to emerge with even greater clarity into your awareness?

Permit images to come into your mind in which that body part is very important. Visualize scenes in which the action centers on that particular body part. Focus on the activity, really get in touch with the body part.

If the images that come to mind have to do with an injury that occurred during your present-life experience, continue to go with that memory until it is played out. Then say to yourself: "That's odd. I remember having injured [the body part] once before in a previous lifetime. I can clearly see myself now as the wound occurs. It happened that time when _____."

Fill in the blank with the first thought that emerges into your consciousness. However far-out it may at first seem to you, permit the thought to grow into a memory of a prior lifetime injury involving the body part that has claimed your attention.

An Exercise for Couples

Sit down facing your friend, lover, mate, child; do not speak. Look at this person for at least two or three minutes. Even if you have looked into those eyes a million times, gaze into them and search their depths.

Truly become aware of the details of the face that is looking back at you. Notice the various colors, textures, shapes, and characteristics of this person's face. Is there any part of the face that seems to attract you more than any other? Is there any part that seems to disturb you?

Fantasize about whichever aspect of the face attracts or annoys you. Try to imagine why you feel as you do. Is there anything happening internally that seems to make it difficult for you to concentrate on your partner's face? Are there any images that seem to be moving into your consciousness? Focus on those images.

As you begin to focus on those competing images, discover if they in any way make you tense or nervous, excited or anticipatory.

Decide which one of you will begin to free-associate first. The one who leads might start by saying such things as, "I remember when we were together before. You looked different then, but I still recognize you. I particularly recognize you because of _____ [spontaneously fill in this blank with whatever occurs to you.] I know that we lived in _____ [name the country, state, city, etc.] in the time or year of _____. I know that our relationship was that of _____ [parent/child, husband/wife, brother/sister, etc.] I know that we have come together in this life experience to complete the lesson of _____ [whatever first comes to mind.]"

When the leader has completed his or her free association, the partner provides whatever confirmation or substantiating details are possible.

If the partner does not relate to the leader's associations, he or she might respond by saying, "I find what you have said to be interesting, but I do not relate to what you have said. Perhaps I remind you of someone of a similar vibration or appearance. However, I believe that I recognize you from a time when we were together before [at this point, the respondent may say something similar to the previously suggested pattern of recognition.]"

Upon completion of the confirmation or the substitute associations, the leader has an opportunity to respond. Sometimes such powerful linkups are established and such potent memories are unlocked through this process that couples continue supplying additional details for several minutes. The experiment need not end until the memory flow ceases.

Awareness Exercises For Family And Friends

Self-awareness and sensitivity activities performed in a gamelike fashion can transform what may have been a dull or normal social evening into an enjoyable and unforgettable experience.

In the following awareness games, the ideal size of the group is six to eight. However, there should be at least four participants and no more than twenty. There are no requirements as to age or sex, and the participants may be friends, family, or total strangers. These games are ideal for "breaking the ice" at any social gathering, for in just a short time people will begin to feel as though they have been friends for years.

We have, however, discovered one factor that should be mentioned here.

In these awareness games people of about the same age seem to relate better to one another. Teenagers feel more comfortable with those under twenty-five, for example, and young adults appear to find it easier to express themselves with their generation. Likewise, mature adults are a bit more communicative with their peers. Of course, within the family these age barriers may be overlooked, for awareness exercises will enable the parents to understand their children better and *vice versa*.

Some people may experience emotional "highs" while participating in these exercises. It seems very natural to the human psyche to release emotions when it has been flooded with a greater awareness or a new insight. This inner "boost" temporarily can be somewhat overwhelming, but it is merely a healthy release, a kind of psychic "cookie" given as a reward for increased understanding and a stimulus to provoke future exploration. A terrific thing about awareness "highs" is that they are the most positive, the most spiritually nurturing, and the most sustaining of all highs.

Those who suffer from anxiety, insomnia, nervousness, headaches, and aches and pains with no discernible physical cause often have found that their symptoms gradually disappear after participating in such awareness techniques as we have outlined in this chapter and the ones we shall describe in detail in the chapter to follow. Many people have described a sense of oneness with a spiritual awakening, a feeling of peace, a beautiful blissfulness, and a kindling of universal love the like of which they have never before experienced.

Whatever it is that you or your participants really desire from life, these awareness exercises may be considered your first step toward that goal, whether it is personal success, more money, more friends, more fame, more pleasure, or a more complete sense of well-being. Greater awareness, which leads to more total self-mastery, is the best and most satisfying way of enjoying life to the fullest.

Begin your sessions by having each member of the group discuss how he or she really feels about life. What is life all about to him or her? What does he or she feel life is like for others? What are this person's ambitions, goals?

Permit very little time to think or to prepare for this exercise. Honesty must be stressed.

Point out at the beginning that anyone who jokes about such a serious subject is revealing something troublesome about his or her own outlook on life. If such a person should persist, it would really be best to exclude him/her from further proceedings. This person may be allowing certain fears and insecurities to inhibit the desire to expand his/her consciousness, and he should not be permitted to impede others' progress toward awareness.

Once the game has begun and some of the participants have given their responses, do not permit anyone merely to agree with what another has stated. Tell that reticent individual that there is much that s/he may lend to the previously voiced opinion. Urge that person to take a moment or two to review the comments, then express his/her personal views on goals, ambitions, the true meaning of life, and so forth.

If someone appears unprepared, he or she should be skipped so that the game is not allowed to bog down. Remember to return to this person later, however.

Never permit any of the participants to argue with another's point of view. An argumentative person will inhibit less aggressive participants. The whole purpose of this opening exercise is to encourage awareness, not establish entrenched opinions through debate.

After each person has taken a turn in expressing his or her belief structure and world view, proceed to the next group awareness exercise.

Ask one or two people to leave the room. While they are

gone, the remaining participants should select an object in the room on which to focus their thoughts. Once the object has been selected, inform them that the object should be the focus of their thoughts, but not their stares or overt attention.

When those who have left the room return, the group should remain silent. Seat the "seekers." Tell them to shut their eyes and attempt to "tune in" on the central thought of the group. Ask them to try to imagine the object. Your seekers should only be told if they are "hot" or "cold" in their guesses until they tune in to the group-focused object.

After each individual has had a turn at being the mental medium, ask your group participants to pair off. (If the numbers are uneven, sets of three may be just as effective.)

Give each individual a pad and a pencil, then dim the lights as completely as is comfortable or practical. Set a candle in the middle of the room. Have your participants seat themselves on the floor so that the flickering images of the candle will be more effective.

Now ask them to stare into one another's eyes. They are to maintain total silence throughout, while at the same time pretending that each is the other. Instruct them to stare into their partner's eyes while practicing comfortable deep breathing for approximately three minutes. Tell them to assume, mentally, their partner's eyes, hair, facial contours, body structure. Ask them to assume the other person's attitudes, responsibilities, personal life. Tell them to become that person.

As the various pairs are attempting to tune into one another, you might be saying such statements and questions as the following:

"Let yourself go into the other person. Feel as though you are that other person. Be that other person.

"Imagine yourself awakening as that person. What duties do you feel that person has to perform during the day? How would he react to situations about which he will feel pleased? How would he react to situations about which he will feel angry? With whom does he interact during the day?

"What does she feel inside about her family, her friends, her life? What kind of past did she have? Happy? Sad? Structured? Chaotic?"

When conducting this exercise with children or young people, insert such questions as these about the future:

"Project this person into the future. What kind of occupation will he have? What kind of mate will he have? How many children will s/he have? What major experiences do you see for her?

For older groups you may adjust future-tense questions as you wish.

The session should be completed in about fifteen to eighteen minutes. Now instruct each individual to write down all that he or she can recall on the notepad you provided.

Silence is imperative. When all have finished recording their recollections, an exchange between groups may begin. Permit this interaction to occur for a few minutes, then begin a group discussion of the exercise. Emphasize the accuracies first. Discourage any negativity, unless it is expressed in lighthearted jesting.

After a brief discussion ask them once again to maintain silence and to stare into their partners' eyes. Ask them this time to visualize that person in a past-life experience.

Ask them if that person was male or female. Ask the name of country, the time sequence, the occupation, trade, or work of that person. Visualize details of that person's life as a husband or wife, brother or sister, child or parent.

Visualize the details of an important experience in that person's past life.

After you have suggested certain aspects to consider, permit a few moments of free association, all the while maintaining silence.

Permit about ten minutes for this exercise, then instruct each individual to write down on the notepad all that s/he can recall about his or her partner's past-life experiences. Follow the same procedures of sharing information.

Object Awareness Fantasy Exercise

Everyone has had the experience of absentmindedly humming a tune over and over until one becomes aware of the title or of a specific snatch of words, then wondering why in the world that song would come to mind so persistently.

Perhaps on a hot evening in July you've found yourself humming "Jingle Bells." Were you, unconsciously, attempting to conjure the crisp chill of a winter's night to absorb some of the summer heat? Or were you feeling nostalgic for a family member whom you always see during the holidays? Perhaps the melody of the song simply makes you feel happy. The image of one particular object or event might present itself to your conscious thinking machine if you were to stop to analyze why you were humming "Jingle Bells" over and over.

Here is an exercise that you might try alone, with one other person, or as a fascinating party game. Encourage your own creative faculties and those of others to fly high and wide and to bring lots of fantasy into play. You can never be certain that what may begin as pure fantasy play might not suddenly take a sharp turn and touch on a very real past-life memory or on a troublesome area in someone's present-life experience.

Let us say that you decide to attempt this exercise as a party game with a group of friends who are at least open to the possibility of past-life memories. First, collect a number of objects, both recognizable and somewhat obscure, both mundane and dramatic. For example, a brightly colored scarf, an ornate comb, a harmonica, a pocket knife, a small statue, a small crystal, a feather, a glove, a pair of old eyeglasses, an ornamental paperweight, and so on. Make sure you have at least one object for each guest who will be at your party.

Place the objects on a table, then by selection or by volunteer, have one of the members step forward and stand silently before the assorted items. Instruct this person in the following manner:

"Allow your awareness to drift from object to object until one of the items begins to stand out more distinctly in your mind. Do not be hasty. Let your awareness wander away from the object for a few moments, then see if your attention directs itself back to the same item.

"When you feel certain that you have focused on the correct object, concentrate on it and permit your thoughts to go deeper into the significance of the item. What is it really like? What is its texture, its composition, its purpose in having been created?

"Now pick it up. Really feel the object in your hand. Allow your concentration to go even deeper into the material essence of the thing.

"Say to yourself, 'I remember an object like this. It was significant to me because [spontaneously say whatever comes to mind]. I remember using it in [country or place] in [year or time]. I remember then that I was [male or female]. I remember that I had [color of eyes] and [color of hair]. I am now looking down at my feet (ask the subject to do so), and I remember wearing [type of shoe or covering] on my feet. I am now looking at my legs, and I remember wearing [describe type of trousers or skirt].'"

Now that you have your subject tuning in on specific details, encourage him or her to continue to free-associate about that particular past-life experience in which the chosen object was significant to him or her. Permit this to go on for a few minutes or as long as the flow is smooth and not interrupted with too many long pauses, then say: "Do you feel that anyone in this room tonight shared that past-life experience with you?" If the subject responds in the affirmative, allow him or her to provide whatever details are forthcoming. Let the person to whom the subject feels a past-life pull have the opportunity to react with his or her impressions.

After all members of your group have had an opportunity to select an object and participate in the game, give them the following advice:

"Do not simply dismiss the experiences of this evening as an entertaining party game. Sometime tonight take the time to analyze or to absorb thoughtfully the impressions that came to you.

"Do not be overly credulous and make sudden and dramatic changes in your life as a result of anything that may have surfaced to your conscious mind. By the same token do not laugh everything away as pure fantasy.

"Consider what occurred tonight as an extended awareness of yourself. You may be able to understand some of the things you said or thought as accurate revelations about certain aspects of your true existence. If you wish to understand deeply all facets of your life, learn to stay in touch with the flow of your awareness."

3

Using Memory as a Tool

We all have experience with memory—recollecting and reminiscing about fleeting, even haunting images of days and moments past. All of our activities are material for memory. The act of remembering is integral to our productive functioning in this reality.

We live in a polarized world. There is a positive as well as a negative aspect to memory and its applications. The positive ways we might use memory need little explanation, for we've all enjoyed exercising this faculty at one time or another. However, the negative application of memory should be understood more clearly, as it can distort our perspective and prove to be our undoing.

If a person allows his perspective toward life to become negative, he will find himself suffering depressions; he will lack ambition, for there will seem to be no hope in furthering himself; and he will feel persecuted as well as victimized by those around him. He will no longer be an effectively contributing member of any relationship.

Yet were it not for the existence of memory we would forget each and every experience the moment after it occurred, and we would not know who we were from one second to the next.

Yes, memory serves as a tool—a tool that you can sharpen. By increasing your ability to remember, and by learning to direct those memories in a positive way, you will be the benefactor of the many blessings a good memory affords you. Memory enhances your capabilities for a more productive life, and a better tomorrow.

Yet it is interesting to note that every past experience consists of many different hues and shades of color. Images of a past event are frequently remembered differently depending on who is doing the remembering. This is not only due to the perspective of the person recording the images, but due to his or her emotional needs as well.

It has been observed that if two or more people view an event dispassionately, though they might not agree on every point, there will at least exist a general consensus as to what really occurred. However, if these very same people became personally and emotionally involved in an event, each one would carry an individual version of it. Each would see it in accordance with his or her own particular needs.

We often change as well as color our memories to comply with our needs. A memory is frequently used to confirm our beliefs, to aid us in supporting our present existing image of ourselves, and to help us survive in our present realities. We view events from the perspective we believe will prove to be the most beneficial to us. Be it a positive or negative perspective, it is based on our own need; and it is our own interpretation of how to meet that need which determines our memories.

Perhaps you've noticed that the recalled event almost always flatters the person who remembers it. It usually places her in a more favorable light or proves that the image of the past she carries with her is an accurate one.

All memories, whether consciously recalled or hidden in the deep recesses of your mind, create the total you. These images will effect you throughout your life.

The memories you *choose* to remember and the perspective from which you view yourself create the more immediate you, the you everyone knows. These selected memories, colored by your needs, give you the image you need in order to function, to survive in your world. However, if the memory of an event does not complement your present self-image, either it will be changed or its contents will be distorted. Or perhaps you will attempt to cover it up altogether so it will not threaten the security of your existing personality or world view.

We must rise above the colorings and distortions of our individual perceptions to become totally aware of the true reality. We must learn to bypass the ego's need to use memory in ways that have little to do with its normal functioning. By facing all of life honestly, without the shackles of ego, we come into the light of awareness.

There is so very much to gain from reviewing your past experiences without the emotion and attachment of ego. By removing the encumbrances of self-image you can begin truly to know yourself. Therefore, you must rise above emotion to permit clarity with which to meet your future. You must give yourself a more balanced perspective on what really exists around you and how it relates to the real you.

We are but one surface of a many-faceted crystal. We are but one facet of a multi-faceted soul, designed to afford us greatest learning with a more balanced perspective and a greater awareness. One lifetime could never afford us the learning and the knowledge required to achieve a truly balanced perspective from which to gain wisdom. As we presently exist, we have a particular perspective that suits our individual needs, and we view and understand all things through that particular perspective.

You will notice that as white light strikes a crystal prism it fractures into a myriad of rainbow-colored hues. Your soul is like a crystal. Each life it has led is but a facet of the whole. Each facet gives off a different hue. Each life you lead affects your perspective and colors your thinking in a particular way.

To continue the analogy of the prism colors, we might

say that a rosy, or happy, life permits us to have a rosy perspective. A blue, or sad, life will afford us a blue perspective.

We must sidestep the "colored" image of an event caused by ego and see it clearly without prejudice or bias. We must experience many lifetimes through soul contact, in order to have a more balanced perspective, thereby attaining the white light that will enable us to view more fully the total reality. All will then be crystal clear. We will be totally aware.

It is as though we came here to Earth long ago with empty arms. We have been gathering the fruits that come from the experiences of living in this physical world. In this way we gain an understanding of love, wisdom, and knowledge through life's experiences. We may one day return to the Source from which we came, our arms heavily laden with the fruits of life.

Let us explore the mind so that we might more fully understand it before we exercise it to its fullest capacity.

Picture a large area that will represent the conscious mind. This area contains all things we deem necessary to function, to exist productively in our present day-to-day reality.

Next, imagine a bridge that connects the conscious mind with another region immediately behind it. This area is a forest known as the subconscious mind.

The strength and width of the bridge determine how easily its owner can cross over to reach into the subconscious mind, where there is a wealth of stored information.

Some people appear to have a weak footbridge that permits only infrequent and difficult crossings and retrievings. Others have a firmly constructed bridge that permits easy crossing and allows frequent visits for drawing gathered information.

It is a strong and wide bridge that supports those who are known for their intelligence, for intelligence is based on memory and the proper use of it. There are many mechanisms that aid in strengthening and widening the bridge that divides your two worlds.

The forest of the subconscious mind is best understood if we imagine that it is reached by following a path or a lane that leads directly from the bridge and goes deep into the forest. On either side of this lane we will discover various images that represent experiences we have had. These images titillate us into stopping and delving deeper into a particular event. These images act as lures or as "barkers" calling out to us to stop and reexperience the entire memory that lies there.

If we stop to heed a call, we will discover a nostalgic play that is ready and waiting for us, complete with scenery and a full cast of characters. All that is necessary is that we, the directors, begin the action by focusing the spotlight of our interest, which stimulates the scene to come alive.

The scene will play itself out according to the dictates of the director. The difference between the truth of the actual experience and the memory of it that is conjured will depend on the director's needs at that particular moment and how s/he chooses to remember him/herself.

There is an interesting phenomenon related to memory that should be discussed. No matter how you might attempt to change a memory, on *some* level of reality it will always remain the same. It always retains its original image and energy. The truth of it always exists in some level of reality and is still known to you.

This truth is what will cause the danger when you attempt to change a past event totally. When you greatly alter a memory, the truth of it will always surface to your conscious mind no matter how you might attempt to drown it. Like a demon it will rear its ugly head when you may be totally unprepared to handle it. This is the grave danger of not facing the total truth.

When a person practices self-deception, she will destroy her own inner strength, her own self-reliance, and thereby will eventually undermine her judgment of all things. She will affect her values and goals and begin, to a greater or lesser degree, to destroy herself.

You must now see the immense value to be gained when you do not practice self-deception but accept the true you. Only when you have done this can you be totally happy and function as a complete person.

The average person strolling down the path of the subconscious mind easily finds those events s/he deems most important. Since they are frequently used, they have gathered little dust. Most of these events are pleasant, and their memory helps make life more complete and enjoyable.

The person whose perspective is imbalanced will find a different subconscious scenario. There will seem to be only events that were painful, unpleasant, or embarrassing; the owner frequently permits these to prey on his mind. Such memories create the desired effect of proving to their owner that life has been terrible, that people have never cared, or that nothing attempted is ever accomplished. Such memories provide the owner with ready-made excuses not to try, to fail. Nothing is worth the effort, so why extend oneself at all? Such memories constitute a poor defense mechanism that is employed by those people whose personal foundation was not as concrete as it should have been or whose life experiences were particularly painful. It is a poor defense mechanism for living, for it leaves one incomplete, depressed, and forever unhappy.

Therefore, it is once again the *perspective* that comes from your chosen self-image that causes you to decide what memory to place in full view, what trimmings shall embellish it, and how it will be utilized to shape your future.

There is valuable wisdom and knowledge to be gained from unhappy experiences. If as a child you suffered through your parents' divorce or even lost contact with one of your parents, you were permitted thereby to know the remaining parent far more intimately than you would have

had the two remained paired. Perhaps both of your parents
died, and this tragedy afforded you the opportunity to come
to know a particular sympathetic relative who later aided in
your further development. Perhaps you lived in many foster
homes, which at the time created chaos in your life, but the
information you gained from diverse personal relationships
became invaluable in your future work.

There is always something to be gained from each and
every painful experience, and if you cannot as yet see it,
perhaps emotion is clouding your vision. You might pretend
that the actual event is happening to someone else, thereby
enabling you, in a more detached way, better to see what the
benefit might be. There is little to be learned by merely
basking in the sun, yet even the lull serves you well, for it
refreshes you and strengthens you to prepare for yet
another period of learning.

It is good practice to balance mentally a painful
experience with the benefit gained from it. Picture the
painful occurrence on the left and its benefits on the right.
You've heard the familiar adage, "Accept the bitter with the
sweet." Balance your bitter experiences with the sweetness
of learning, for therein lies wisdom.

It is important to take meaningful strolls down the path
of your most prominent memories. Go back into your past
year by year. Search out and relive each and every experience
you can discover. This is best accomplished by first quieting
yourself and drifting into your own mind.

Envision first the area of the conscious mind that
contains such facts as phone numbers, addresses, places of
occupation, people valuable to your life, and so on. Approach
the bridge that connects your two worlds. Notice it carefully.
Is it small, narrow, weak? Do you have to leap across to the
other side? Or is the bridge sturdy, wide enough to permit a
caravan of information to travel across from the other side?
Cross over and be mindful of the importance of your mission
at hand. Set about your task positively and with the

certainty that you are about to accomplish a great deal.

Here is a little play we'll enact for purpose of illustration. Our illustrative drama will demonstrate how we often change, not only the scene, but sometimes the actual event itself. Learn to see memory scenes the way they truly occurred and to understand your relationship to them in order to benefit fully from your mental memory excursions. Facing the truth about your past can only be beneficial and should only be accomplished after the sting has passed, the emotion is gone. If, however, you choose for whatever reason not to face an event, continue on to the next event. Perhaps one day you will escape the experience's hold on you, see it for what it really was, and thereby gain fully from the memory.

As we shall demonstrate repeatedly in this book, facing the truth of remembered events will not only sharpen your memory, but will benefit you in innumerable ways.

Our dramatized memory is of an individual who changed the memory of an event to create a better self-image (or so she thought). This distorted memory helped its owner to prove that she had been admired by her peers. Yet in truth the energy from the actual memory surfaced disturbingly throughout her life, echoing from the dark recesses of her mind, for truth can never be covered up fully. Imagine yourself in her situation.

There was a gathering of about one hundred students in the high school cafeteria. They had decided to distribute a petition and submit it to the school board in an attempt to convince a favorite teacher that he should not leave, and to advise his replacement that he should not stay. They hoped that as a result of their petition the school board might increase Coach Barbella's salary as an inducement not to accept a lucrative position outside of the scholastic system. Since Barbella was the coach of the winning football team, all the popular students—the jocks, cheerleaders, and so on—were championing the petition. They announced loudly to all the students gathered that Coach Barbella was the best teacher and coach in the entire city. The new coach, an unknown, would probably lead them into their greatest losses.

The petition was then circulated. It was easy for the popular students to intimidate the others, for if a student were not grateful enough at having been approached and even spoken to by one of the elite, a haughty glare or a muscular arm planted firmly on the student's table would soon prompt him to conform and sign.

The paper reached you bearing almost all the signatures needed. You defiantly rose, gathering the nerve necessary to support your convictions about giving the new coach a chance while the petition lay ignored on your desk.

Addressing your peers you said, "Let's at least show we have given the new teacher the benefit of the doubt. If he's as bad as some kids fear, we'll know it in a few weeks, then we can petition him out. Coach Barbella would feel it was only fair play!"

All those students gathered around you began discussing your plea with one another and then unanimously agreed with your decision.

The new teacher proved to be every bit as excellent a coach as Coach Barbella, and he led the school team to become All City Champs. Nearly all the students remembered your contribution throughout high school.

Look deep into the memory of this event; walk around it and examine it on all sides. Buried in the thick underbrush of the subconscious is the truth of the experience.

You are in the "unpopular" homeroom. It is five minutes or so before the school bell rings and homeroom begins. There is no teacher present yet. The door opens and in steps the captain of the football team, followed by the high scorer, the cheerleaders they are dating, and two of their followers. The captain raises a long sheet of paper overhead and announces in a strong, self-assured voice, "Coach Barbella is leaving! He's the greatest coach this school has ever known! Sign this petition to keep out this new guy, Clark, and get Barbella to stay."

The petition is entitled "We Want Barbella," and it is placed on one student's desk. He is instructed to sign it and pass it on. The football players promise to return after homeroom to retrieve the signed petition. "Don't let the teacher see this!" they further instruct, then leave.

About fifteen minutes into homeroom the petition, now folded, has been gingerly passed from one student to another, and it is finally placed in silence on your desk. It never goes any farther. You aren't going to sign it. You have decided not to take orders from a group of people who, any other day of the year, act as though you don't exist, let alone count. You feel an empathy for the new teacher, Clark. He is like you. He doesn't count either. He isn't accepted by the popular kids. Therefore, you don't sign the petition and you never pass it on. Instead you whisper to your friend that you aren't about to sign it.

When homeroom bell rings and all are leaving, you explain to your friend how you really feel. Perhaps one or two other people passing by overhear you. You aren't really certain. Everyone leaves and no one remains to explain the missing petition to the football players.

Whether other petitions circulated throughout the school and were submitted or not, you never heard. The facts remained and were: Coach Clark stayed on, was an excellent teacher, and led the team to win the All City trophy. Coach Barbella left to supervise an insurance company, and you and your girl friend remembered your act of courage throughout high school.

We believe that it is easier to face the future once we have come to terms with the past. If for reasons of face-saving and self-preservation, whether real or imagined, you have been falsifying your memories of a certain past event, we feel that it is important that you face the truth about the matter and recognize just how things really were. One of the most important concepts we wish to share with you is that of internal honesty. By remaining truthful with yourself about the actual reality of your past, you will have a much better chance of building a more positive tomorrow. And the more positive your future appears, the more deeply you can freely delve into the past.

Using Color Visualization To Relax The Body And Free The Memory

The color visualization process is a very simple and effective relaxation technique we have often used with great success. This technique involves occasional deep breathing and the visualization of various colors. It has the advantage of serving as an effective tranquilizer whenever you feel yourself succumbing to tension.

Sit or lie in a comfortable position in a place where you will not be disturbed for some time. Relax. Take a few deep breaths, then....

Visualize that at your feet lies a blanket the color *rose*. It has been determined by researchers in the United States and in certain European and Asian nations that the color rose stimulates natural body warmth and induces sleep. It also provides you with a sense of well-being and a feeling of being loved.

Imagine that you are now pulling a rose-colored, blanket-like aura slowly over your body. Feel it moving over your feet, up your legs, over your stomach, your chest, your arms, your neck; then, making a comfortable hood of the cover, imagine that you bring it up over your head.

The color *green* serves as a disinfectant, a cleanser. It also influences the proper building of muscle and tissue.

Imagine that you are pulling a green blanket-like aura over your body. Feel it moving over your feet, cleansing, healing them of all pains and ills. Feel the green aura moving up your legs, cleansing, healing. Feel it moving over your stomach, your chest, your arms, your neck; then, making a comfortable hood of the green cover, bring it up over your head.

Gold has been noted to be a great strengthener of the nervous system. It also aids digestion and helps you become calm.

Visualize now that you are pulling a soft, beautiful gold blanket-like aura slowly over your body. Feel it moving over your chest, your arms, your neck; then, making a comfortable hood of the gold cover, bring it up over your head.

Researchers have discovered that *red-orange* strengthens and cleanses the lungs. In our modern society with its problems of pollution, our lungs become fouled whether we smoke cigarettes or not. Yogis and other masters have long known that effective meditation, effective altered states of consciousness, can best be achieved through proper techniques of breathing, through clean lungs.

Imagine before you a red-orange cloud of pure oxygen. Take a comfortably deep breath and visualize some of that orange cloud moving into your lungs.

Imagine it traveling through your lungs, cleansing away particles of impurities. Visualize yourself exhaling that red-orange cloud from your lungs. See how soiled with impurities it is.

Take another comfortably deep breath. See again the red-orange cloud moving through your lungs, purifying them of the effects of smoke, exhaust fumes, industrial gases. Breathe again of the purifying cleansing red-orange cloud.

The color *yellow-orange* will aid oxygen in moving into every organ and gland of your body, purifying them, cleansing them.

Imagine before you now a yellow-orange cloud of pure oxygen. Take a comfortable deep breath and pull that cleansing, purifying yellow-orange cloud into your lungs. Feel it moving through your body. Feel it cleansing and purifying every organ. If you have any area of weakness or disease, feel the yellow-orange energy bathing it in cleansing vibrations.

Now exhale all impurities. Inhale again and visualize the cleansing process throughout your body. Exhale, then inhale again, seeing your body become pure and clean.

See now that the cloud you exhale is as clean and as pure as that which is being inhaled. You have cleansed and purified your lungs. You have cleansed and purified your body and all of its organs.

The color *violet* serves as an excellent muscle relaxer. Violet is a tranquilizer. It is a color of the highest vibration. Violet will help you to sleep.

Imagine that you are slowly pulling a blanket-like aura of violet over your body. Feel it moving over your feet, relaxing you, soothing you, calming you. Feel it moving over your stomach, your chest, your arms, your neck; then, making a comfortable hood of the violet cover, bring it over your head.

Blue is the color of psychic ability, the color that increases visionary potential.

Visualize a blue blanket-like aura beginning to move over your body. Feel it moving over your feet, relaxing them, soothing them. Feel it moving, bring it over your head.

You are now sitting or lying in your blue cover. You are very secure, very comfortable, very relaxed. Your mind is very receptive, very aware.

You are now ready to explore deep, deep within you and to receive knowledge of past lives.

Visualize a blue blanket-like aura beginning to move over your body. Feel it moving over your feet, relaxing them, soothing them. Feel it movinp within you and
to receive knowledge of past lives.

Statue Projection Exercise

Practice a yogic breathing or color processing technique to place yourself in a state of reverie and receptivity.

Visualize yourself walking through a great and magnificent temple in some other dimension of being. This temple is dedicated to artistic representations of the soul and its various expressions throughout history. As you turn a corner, you suddenly confront a statue of yourself as you looked in an important past-life experience.

Imagine the statue before you. Even though the figure may not greatly resemble you in your present-life experience, you are certain beyond all doubt that it is really you.

Of what material has the statue been made?

How large is the statue?

In what pose has the statue been fashioned? What is the figure doing?

Is the figure male or female?

From what you can assume, in what field of thought, endeavor, or accomplishment did the figure excel?

Now study the statue carefully. Feel yourself becoming one with the statue. Feel yourself breathing life and warmth into the statue. See yourself reliving the important events of that lifetime which resulted in a statue's being made in your likeness.

In what country or place and in what historical time did you live?

What was your greatest ambition in that lifetime? What did you want most to accomplish?

Now visualize scenes of conflict, scenes of strife. See if you sense or perceive anyone from your present-life experience striving against you in that lifetime. If you recognize anyone at all, take a few moments to contemplate what lesson you see here that can help resolve some aspect of your present-life experience.

Now see if you sense or perceive anyone from your

present-life experience who is championing you, supporting you, working with you in those scenes of strife and chaos. If you recognize anyone at all, take a few moments to contemplate why you have come together again in your current lifetime.

Scan that lifetime and visualize the events of greatest conflict. After you have reflected upon these situations for a few moments, imagine the events and occasions of your greatest triumphs.

Did you achieve your goal in that lifetime?

How did you die?

What was the most important lesson that you learned from that lifetime?

What situations would you most like to redo in that lifetime? What patterns of behavior would you least wish to replicate?

Past Life Companion Exercise

Lie or sit in a comfortable position and allow yourself to relax as completely as possible. Take a deep breath, hold it for the count of three, then slowly exhale. Repeat this procedure three times.

Visualize yourself sitting or reclining in your favorite place. Perhaps on a blanket on the beach. Perhaps on a rock beside a lovely mountain trail, or on a park bench feeding the pigeons. On a comfortable couch in your own home. Wherever you choose to imagine yourself. Next visualize that you have a companion with you.

Focus on this companion. Is the companion male or female? Study the color of hair, eyes, and complexion of your companion.

Watch your companion's facial expressions, posture, body movements. Are you relaxed with your companion? Is he or she relaxed with you?

If there is an instant rapport between you, take a few

moments to learn why you feel so much at ease with one another.

If there is veiled hostility or distrust between you, take a few moments to contemplate the possible origin of those feelings.

Really focus now on your companion's face. Have you known this companion before in this present lifetime, or is this companion only a vaguely familiar stranger?

If you have visualized a person whom you know from your present-life experience, take a few moments to flow with your feelings. Who might this person represent?

It is quite likely that you have visualized your companion in contemporary clothing. If this is true, now that you are beginning to move into deeper thoughts about your companion, visualize him or her in clothing that you think most perfectly suits the individual. Permit this costuming to come from any period in history. Do not place any restraints on the flow that may now be coming to you.

Now visualize yourself with your companion in another time, another place. If your prior selection of beach, mountain trail, park bench, or home feels significant, however, stay with that environment. Imagine yourself taking your companion by the hand as you face an audience or circle of friends and make an introduction along the following lines:

"I would like you to meet my companion . We lived together in [country] in [year]. Our relationship was [marriage partners, business partners, comrades-in-arms, siblings, whatever].

"Together, we faced [a situation of conflict]. We shared bad times [reflect upon some] and good times [enjoy positive memories]. Our life together as companions ended when [remember the circumstances—death, separation, anger, whatever]. The most important lesson we learned together was [recall why you lived that past life together]."

4

The Many Faces of Reincarnation

She was "sweet sixteen," at least that's how we found her to be, although her parents complained otherwise. Attractive and shy, a reluctant Gayle was ushered into our waiting area by her distraught parents.

We could see the obvious tension that existed among the three of them. Gayle was their only daughter, though they had two sons, one older, the other considerably younger.

The only way to get a true picture of the bizarre story that had been hurriedly relayed to us over the telephone was to discuss quietly with each of them the entire matter from beginning to end.

The father said he knew little about the whole story, but he was at his wit's end to know what to do. He explained how the entire situation went against all of his religious training. They were Southern Baptist and things of this nature seemed to be something from the devil himself. The only reason he consented to bring Gayle to us was that it was the proverbial last straw. Actually, he said, he preferred our discussing the entire matter with his wife, who knew far more than he about the "mess."

The distraught mother was the easiest of the three to talk to. She poured out her heart to us. Gayle had always been a loving child, an "A" student, had involved herself in many school activities, and had always been a very popular, well-liked girl.

The tragedy had begun almost a year before when Gayle began telling her mother about dreams in which she saw the face of a young man she had known somewhere, long, long ago. She knew she deeply loved him, but somehow they had parted.

The mother didn't think much of the dreams until Gayle began acting in contrast to her normal, cheerful self. Many mornings upon awakening she would appear as though she had been crying. Questioned, she would deny it, saying her eyes were just tired.

Gayle had always been an eight-hour sleeper, but she now began to sleep ten hours or more a day. She began going to bed early, rather than spending evenings out with her friends.

Her mother had suggested a physical checkup to discover why she slept so late and why she was overly tired, but Gayle said, "No, I've not been sleeping, I've been reading by my night light!"

Overlooking a ten-pound weight loss in the hope that Gayle would pull out of the strange habit pattern and change back to her usual self, the mother let it continue for another month—until she heard Gayle sobbing long into the night. When she awakened her, the girl poured out the entire story amidst tearful sobs.

The dream was the same each night. She kept a vigil for her loved one, waiting for his return. She died waiting for him, never to see his beautiful face again.

The mother sobbed uncontrollably; she had been under severe stress, and it took several minutes after she told us about Gayle's dreams before we could calm her and return her to her family. She told us that several ministers and therapists had been sought to no avail.

Gayle reluctantly entered our office, lay down on the couch with a resigned bounce. She eyed us with distrust. Getting her to relax was no easy matter. Several distraction techniques, interspersed with understanding smiles and soft words, made her feel more able to confide in us.

Every night while in the dream state Gayle would find herself standing before a mirror in what appeared to be her bedroom. Her image was quite different from her present appearance. Her hair was long and dark and it hung in natural curls over her shoulders. She was wearing a beautiful green dress in the style of someone living in the sixteenth or seventeenth century. She was primping, applying a tiny bit of coloring to her cheeks and mouth, powdering her face a bit. She was preparing herself to meet someone very important to her, someone she loved.

She had no sooner finished her preparations when she heard horses and men outside the window. Sharp hooves clicking on the cobblestones announced the arrival of many soldiers returning home from battle. She could hear the happy cheers of throngs of people gathered to greet them.

Rushing to the window beside her bed, she looked down to the street below. Her eyes vainly searched through the parade of bedraggled, happy-faced warriors. Her lover had to be there. Surely she would soon see him.

Her heart pounded in her chest. Life seemed to stand still until she could once again see his face. She thought of his curly blond hair, shining in the sun, his blue eyes looking into hers.

No longer able to control herself, she ran out to the streets below to find him. Pushing and shoving through the loud, cheering crowd was no easy feat. The line of men on horseback seemed endless. At least an hour passed before she had searched the faces of all present, coming to the very last of the soldiers.

She began to retrace her steps, this time calling out his name, "David! David!" She called until her throat became dry and parched. But her loved one wasn't among the returning soldiers. Two of his friends dismounted and approached her. They told of David's being taken captive by the enemy. They had struggled to prevent his capture, but they had barely escaped with their lives. They sadly informed her that he was gravely wounded and had probably not survived the journey to the enemy's camp.

The two men described how David had valiantly called out to them to say that they must return home and tell his beloved that he had died courageously in battle, so she would not wait for him forever. David had believed that he would soon be dead.

She stumbled away, dazed, to walk aimlessly the entire night. By morning her clothes were wet from the dew.

Days, weeks, and months seemed to pass, and she knew she was eating less, growing weaker, thinner. She had been unable to shake a cough that had grown progressively worse. Gayle felt perhaps that she had died, never having seen David again.

The dream was forever the same, etched now into her mind. Each night she would be standing before the mirror, wearing the same green dress, listening to the horses' hooves clicking outside her window. She knew she would run through the crowd, never seeing her lover's face. Two of his friends would say those same words over and over to her. "He was taken captive. He is probably dead." She would wait anyway. Days, weeks, months would pass, and she felt she was slowly dying, perhaps starving to death, or perhaps she had pneumonia—Gayle wasn't certain. The last scene of her dream was the faint sketch of her lover's face.

Gayle would awaken before she could find out if she ever saw David again. She awakened crying, half from a past-related emotion, half from frustration.

As Gayle told the story to us, her brown eyes brimmed with tears. She felt she couldn't take it anymore. She wanted to sleep without dreaming. Yet she wanted to know if she might ever see her former loved one again.

Reincarnation was a forbidden word in her home. If it was not she, who was the girl in the green dress with whom she so identified?

We felt we could help her. We excused ourselves to rejoin her parents in our waiting room, leaving Gayle lying quietly, relaxing.

We explained to them what we were going to attempt, asking them to please read a particular chapter of a book Francie had written, *Reflections from an Angel's Eye,* that would explain the belief we shared on reincarnation.

We excused ourselves while they read it, refreshed ourselves for the journey on which we felt we would soon embark. We knew the parents had few alternatives. The several therapists and ministers they had sought had only confused Gayle, leaving her in a dire state of need.

Minutes later we passed through the waiting area to rejoin Gayle, checking with her parents to see if they were willing for us to continue. They agreed to let us try.

We hurriedly rejoined Gayle to deliver the good news. She was a willing, happy subject. She knew she would receive an answer to her many disturbing dreams, as well as see the former loved one once again. She wanted desperately to know if the girl in the green dress was she, if she really died without seeing David again.

We relaxed her, using a ten-minute technique, our voices echoing one another. Soon she stood before the mirror, dressed in the beautiful long dress. Her name was Anne. We hurried her through the dream to the point where much time had passed. David had never returned and she was in bed, unable to walk, quite ill.

A neighbor named Lena, a widow quite old, had come to care for her. She fixed her a soup made with beaten eggs and small vegetables. Soon Lena was spending more time with Anne than in her own small hovel of a home, and she nursed Anne back to health.

Lena didn't need much coercion to move in with Anne,

and the two became constant companions. Anne had lived alone since she was fifteen. She was now nineteen, and her parents had been dead for the past four years. Lena had always wanted children yet she had been barren. Anne was the daughter she had longed for.

A year passed and they had acquired a small dog, one that had been deserted, as alone as each of them had been. One night when the dog began barking, Anne awakened to a hurried rap on the door. Lena, too, had been roused, and both women and the dog stood before the open door to greet a dirty, bedraggled young man.

David! He had escaped. He was back. Anne had known in her heart he would return.

We watched as tears slipped from Gayle's eyes and a broad smile stretched across her face. "David, David!" she kept saying.

We let her experience the entire lifetime more hurriedly so she might view it in full, then we awakened her. Gayle was ecstatic with joy. She hugged us both, kissing us, holding us, and crying.

She told us how Anne had waited until David returned, how he came to her one dark, wet night having escaped from his captors. Anne married David and had three beautiful children—two boys and a girl—and Lena became the perfect grandmother.

In later years Lena passed on. Anne led a wondrously happy life with David until she was eighty-four years old. Gayle told us of Anne's dying, of passing right through the ceiling of their room, entering into another dimension, seeing a most beautiful land with wonderful people. Then she awakened.

Gayle told us how she felt a kinship, a sort of sistership with Anne, that they were somehow related; but more than that, she felt personally affected by her.

When we brought out the happy Gayle, whose smiling face had been but a memory for almost a year, her parents began to cry. Actually we all cried, and we believe you would have, too, had you been present.

The rewards of being able to help people get their lives together in the here and now are very gratifying. Although we bring to such consultations more than forty years of combined experience, the enormous demand for our services as past-life regressionists has recently forced us to discontinue seeing people on an individual basis. We have, however, carefully devised a series of tape cassettes that faithfully re-create these powerful awareness experiences in the privacy and security of one's own environment. At the same time we still conduct past-life and awareness seminars throughout the country, and these seminars, together with the cassettes and books such as this one, continue our public mission.

At this point we should discuss various other approaches to the subject of reincarnation, as well as provide you with our *own* interpretation of the evolution of the Soul.

In an earlier work, *You Will Live Again* (Dell Books), we asked our friend and longtime hypnotic regressionist, Dick Sutphen, to provide us with an analysis of various concepts of the promise of rebirth and his interpretations of the theories of other researchers. We feel that section from chapter 20, "The Goal of Rebirth," bears a slightly condensed repeating.

Spiritual Lineage Concept: You have never been anyone else, and you will never be anyone else. Yet you carry in your subconscious mind the spiritual essence of others who have lived before you. When you are hypnotically regressed into a previous lifetime, you are actually reliving the life of *your* creator.

As an example, in regression you see yourself as an Englishman in 1850. The man actually lived and died in that time period; after crossing over into the nonphysical realms, *he* created you as an extension of his own identity to further explore Earthly incarnations. His "spiritual essence" was introduced into you when you were but a fetus; thus, you are an extension of him.

He is not controlling you, for once anything is created it is freed; but rather he is feeling and experiencing everything through you. His karma, good or bad, is your karma. When you cross over to the other side, you will have the same opportunity to experience through others who will take on your karma...

Simultaneous Multiple Incarnations (Parallel Lives): The Earth's spiritual vibrations are accelerating, and as they do, more and more "old souls" (souls who have experienced several previous physical expressions) will cross over into the material world as bodies become available. These souls are very experienced and have the ability to inhabit more than one body at a time. They seek to accelerate the evolutionary process by exploring as many lives as possible within the shortest time frame.

It may be that, as the population of the world grows larger, it is actually growing smaller from a "soul count perspective." In other words, there are fewer souls, but as the frequencies continue to intensify, it will be the highly advanced souls who cross over to inhabit even larger numbers of bodies at the *same* time.

Lack Of Time Concept: There is no such thing as time; all of our lives—past, present, and future—are being lived at the *same* moment. Each historic period exists on the Earth within a different frequency of Time/Space, and thus each is invisible and untouchable to the others. Time is a concept that relates to your perception, from your birth up until this moment.

If this concept is valid your past lives are affecting you, but you are also affecting your past lives in the way you perceive them. The same is true, of course, for the future...

The Oversoul Concept: The very essence of your soul exists as an "Oversoul" on the other side, possibly on a Godhead level. Physical lifetimes are lived as a form of procreation and expansion of the Oversoul energy. You are like a cell in the body of your God-level totality—the part and the whole at the same time...The Oversoul could conceivably be exploring billions of potentials at the same time.

To better understand the part-and-whole concept, think of a single cell within your body. It contains your complete "pattern." If our human cloning abilities were developed, as they are with some reptiles, you could be "duplicated" from that cell.

Projecting the concept from a superconscious level, you have all of the knowledge of your Oversoul, or God totality. That knowledge may exist in the 95 percent of mind that is not normally used.

The Total Illusion Concept: Life is an illusion, a game, created as an evolutionary process of the soul—or maybe—simply for the fun of it. You are God. You created the entire environment (world) to make the game seem real and to give you limitless possibilities for exploration and growth. Maybe everybody else actually exists, but maybe they are only illusions...

The Classic Concept: Reincarnation is an evolving process of physical exploration of the perfection of the soul, a system of total justice and balance. We learn needed lessons through Karma (cause and effect) and carry this intuitive knowledge with us through successive incarnations. Each entity is born into each new Earth life with a level of awareness (vibrational rate) established in past lives. How the lifetime is lived will dictate whether the rate is raised or lowered.

In the nonphysical realms of "the other side" there are seven levels. Each successive level is more desirable, with the top level being the God-level, or Godhead. It is our vibrational rate which dictates our level after death. The entity, upon crossing over, will seek the level of his or her own rate, but will be unable to remain in the more intense upper levels.

Due to our desire to perfect our soul, and thus to return

to the Godhead, we reincarnate in successive Earth lives in hopes of using our past-life knowledge to live a "good" physical life. In so doing, we will raise our vibrational rate, moving closer to our "soul-goal" of returning to God.

The concept of reincarnation that works best for us was received in two ways. After having participated in hundreds of individual regressions over a twelve year period, Brad believed that he had arrived at the "facet of soul" theory through his own intellectual process. Francie, on the other hand, was given basically the same concept by her master teacher, who presented her with a living diagram in the timeless realm where visions live.

Brad had concluded that rather than each *personality* going through reincarnation again and again in order to learn and to progress on Earth's plane, perhaps there was a soul-in-common for several physical personalities that materially manifest in subsequent incarnations.

Let us say, for example, that you seem to recall a life as a Roman soldier *circa* 100 B.C.; a lifetime as a Persian trader *circa* A.D. 300; a time as a Viking raider *circa* A.D. 1000; an existence as a crusader A.D. 1100; and a rugged experience as a pioneer woman *circa* 1873.

It may be that you did not literally live those former life experiences as the *same* essential personality being reborn. Your present self-manifestation is able to tap into memories of growth and spiritual evolution that have been absorbed by a *common* soul.

In this theory, the soul may have materially expressed itself in hundreds of lifetimes and will have assimilated the growth memories from each of those physical manifestations. But each of those individual personalities has lived only once.

It may be that the particular lessons learned by the Persian trader, the Crusader, and the Roman legionnaire have all contributed valuable essences to your present-life experience.

It may be that specific memories from your soul's former expression as a Viking raider are causing certain difficulties in the present.

It also may be that the life as a pioneer woman is the one that is most closely connected to your present-life experience in terms of certain "seeds" you are reaping today.

But you were not actually *any* of those individuals in a previous-life experience. You are only able to tune in to certain memory cells of spiritual knowledge in the common soul. Properly utilized, this ability to tap into the common soul can aid you in acquiring wisdom and increased growth in your present lifetime.

And now for your consideration we are presenting the vision experience of the soul and its expressions that Francie received in the timeless realm:

"I was taken from my physical body to a realm far out in space where I stood suspended. A living panorama was brought before me, a moving diagram, which provided me with many levels of awareness. I was shown an area in the upper right-hand region and I was told that it was a realm beyond ours, a space occupied by the Source, God.

"A golden cord extended down from that realm to the higher self, the soul, which was represented by a large glowing sphere. The golden cord was the umbilical cord that connects our higher self with God. The golden cord is our lifeline to the Source.

"Extending from the higher self were many silver cords which formed starlike rays in every direction. They, too, were "umbilical cords" that connected each lifeform that the soul had entered. At the end of each silver cord there existed smaller crystal-like spheres, approximately twelve in number, which I was told represented each lifetime led on Earth.

"As I watched, an embryo formed within each of the spheres. The embryo became a child and matured to various ages. While each lifeform matured, it gathered knowledge, which was represented by sparkling lights around the sphere. Corresponding lights also became incorporated into the body known as the soul, which was located at the hub of the model. The appearance was as a starburst. As the lifeform grew in awareness, so, equally, did the higher self, the soul. And as the lights came to be within the soul, it grew to a more brilliant, vibrating intensity of white light. I "knew" its vibrations had increased from the knowledge gained by the human lifeform.

"Upon the death of the lifeforms I saw that some of the spirits within automatically became incorporated into the soul, for they had been vibrating at a similar higher rate of awareness. Other lifeforms, vibrating at a lesser rate, simply grew dark.

"This process continued throughout time, until all motion ceased. By then the soul had grown brilliant and was pulsating rapidly with the highest energies. It was magnificent to behold, as if it were a god.

"I was told that all souls continue in this fashion, gathering vibrations, until they raise their *own* energies with the many experiences gained from the various human lifeforms. The souls thereby eventually return to the Highest Vibration, the Source, more enriched from their many experiences than when they were first created and sent forth.

"The *judgment* of each lifeform, which determines whether it will be incorporated into the soul to be as a god, is a self-judgment. Either we vibrate with the higher awareness gained from the wisdom of experience, or we remain ignorant. It is our own choice.

"Those lifeforms that raised their vibrations, their awareness, were automatically incorporated into their soul upon physical death. They will be one with the soul in its ascent to the Source.

"Those lifeforms that had chosen ignorance remained dark, barely pulsating with energy. They were unable to become incorporated into the soul. There must then be another system by which all those who did not become incorporated into their soul will rejoin the Source.

"The relationship between our higher self and our spirit within us is of a symbiotic nature. The soul needs us as much as we need it. Through awareness gained from meditation and experience we can raise our vibrations, become as one with our soul, and ascend with it to the Source of all energy.

"For in the beginning the Source sent forth essences of itself, androgynous souls, the first of all creation. These essences of intelligent energy were connected by a golden umbilical-like cord.

"In like manner and for the purpose of furthering creation, some androgynous souls descended from the realm of the Source. Splitting, they became male and female. Essences from *their* beings were sent forth into the dimension of physical matter, thus entering humankind. We are spirits within fleshly bodies and we are connected to our soul by a silver cord.

"Through experiences on the Earth plane, we gather many learnings, many memories as well as the higher vibrations of love, wisdom, and knowledge. These beneficial vibrations are received simultaneously by our soul through the silver umbilical-like cord.

"Through meditation and the higher vibrations gained from spiritual life experiences, we establish a strong bond with our soul. In doing this we not only gain access to the wealth of memories from the former lifetimes of the soul, we find that our own life on Earth is transformed into one of purpose, productivity, and fulfillment of our destiny, for we are reflecting the wishes of our soul.

"We have all met people who reflect their soul, as well as those who do not—those who live as though they were stillborn, without purpose or destiny.

"Certain phobias, memories, and circumstances exist because we as individuals balance the former expression of our soul. The soul chooses certain environmental and personal conditions to exist for our present-life expression to balance the emanations from the former soul-chosen existence. It is the soul's responsibility to balance the vibrations that compromise each life led, for all energy and all matter are bound by the law of polarities when they exist in this dimension.

"Upon the death of our Earthly flesh, if we (our inner spirits) are vibrating at a high frequency, we will automatically be incorporated into our soul. This incorporation will seem like Heaven to us. Ultimately, however, we will ascend with our soul when it returns to the eternal Heaven, the realm of the Source, heavy laden, bearing the fruits received from its many experiences. In this way the Source is magnified, glorified, increased in greatness."

At this point in his quest Dick Sutphen, author of *You Were Born To Be Together* and *Past Lives, Future Loves*, believes the greatest value in discovering information about one's past lives is "anxiety reduction." Dick and his wife, Trenna, agree with psychiatrist Dr. David Viscott, who observed: "All feelings come from some definite event, even if that event cannot be clearly defined or located in time."

Dick and Trenna feel that if they can help a person know the cause of a problem situation—a hangup, a fear, a phobia, et cetera—they can sometimes eliminate the effect.

Their favorite techniques for helping another person remember an important past-life experience are 1) directed past-life hypnotic regression, 2) self-hypnosis, 3) pre-recorded regression tapes, 4) assertive directed meditation, 5) dream programming, 6) various self-channeling techniques, such as automatic writing, the pendulum, verbal channeling, 7) going to a good psychic.

After five years of conducting seminars on reincarnation as a possible explanation of life problems, Dick presently thinks Zen gives him great mental peace:

"Zen incorporates the concept of reincarnation and Karma without dogma. 'You forged the chains for your enslavement and you can break them. If you are looking for miracles, look within, not without'.

"I see Zen as neither a philosophy nor a religion, but a process of liberation. It begins with the assumption that there is nothing to seek and nothing to find. The seeker is already enlightened and no one can give him what he already has. The wise man is concerned with becoming aware of what he already is, the True Self within, and to accept his own perfection."

Karma, in the view of the Sutphens, is a cause-and-effect system that brings about self-inflicted problems based on prior programming. According to their *Master of Life Manual*:

"If the subconscious were to receive no new programming, it would continue to operate on past input. This, of course, cannot happen, for you are constantly feeding new programming or data into your subconscious mind—your computer. Every thought programs the computer. Thus, if you are thinking negatively more than positively, you are programming your computer in the wrong way. You create your own reality or Karma, with your thoughts."

Dick and Trenna's truth is that "...wisdom erases Karma.

"You have a choice of living in response to your previous programming or of choosing to take control of your life and use wisdom to create your own reality."

"It appears that living is a series of things to handle," Dick reflected, "and to make it interesting, we give some things more importance than others. Thus we create goals/games. Everything we do is really a game, and most people are playing a lot of games they never consciously chose to play. They don't even like most of the games in their life.

"For me, life works better when I create what I desire to experience. I prefer to play games that are appropriate and fun and relate to my chosen purpose."

Dame Sybil Leek, author of numerous best-selling books on reincarnation and metaphysics and a long-time personal friend, believes that spontaneous recall of past lives comes only when we need such memories. Careful hypnosis is her favorite technique for assisting one in remembering an important past-life experience.

Dame Sybil cannot remember a time when she did not accept the concept of reincarnation. "The acceptance was rather shallow in my youth," she told us, "and then in a momentous 'revelation,' which I cannot explain, I knew that it was an inevitable truth.

"I feel my whole life—now that I have lived long enough to review it—has been one long testimony of reincarnation. I can tap into so many things which I have never studied. Always when I need to know anything, it will be there. The memory of past experiences will flood in for me to pick and choose what I need for any specific time."

Dame Sybil spoke to the question of "old souls" and "new souls," by commenting: "There must be old souls and very new souls in each sequence of incarnations. It seems so obvious to me that some low spiritually evolved types come to their first human experience as an individual from a group spirit of animals and birds; and they often have only animal memories to draw on, hence animalistic instincts prevail."

It is not difficult for Dame Sybil to conceive that the evolution of souls may also exist on many levels. "Certainly, fragments of ourselves *could exist on extraterrestrial or multidimensional levels.* Perhaps this is why we have to look for some missing 'parts' of ourselves. This is a *belief.* I have not researched it, but it seems logical."

In Dame Sybil's cosmology everyone reincarnates. "There is no rule for one and not for others. It is the *time* one reincarnates and the *level* at which one reincarnates that matters."

Karma, to her, has nothing to do with punishment. "It's your chance to make good your past mistakes and to travel on toward perfection."

Dame Sybil is well aware of several guides with whom she interacts, both in exploring past lives and in her daily existence. "I have never had one consistent guide, but there are many who 'tune in' when they can be helpful for a specific purpose. It is great to have one's own advisory council!"

Dr. Hemendra Nath Banerjee of the Center for Para-Analytical Studies, San Diego, California, has traveled around the world more than sixty times in twenty-five years to authenticate over one thousand cases of reincarnation. Dr. Banerjee has become a trusted friend in the fifteen years that we have been in communication. He prefers to use the term "Extra Cerebral Memory" to describe such cases, because he wishes to be totally objective in his research. For an empirical scientist the term "reincarnation" implies certain philosophical or spiritual assumptions.

But that slight scientific prejudice aside, "Hem," as we know him, speaks freely of reincarnation. Whether one terms the experience reincarnation or Extra Cerebral Memory, Dr. Hem Banerjee accepts without any shadow of doubt that it is true.

In a paper presented to the Fifth International Congress of Psychosomatic Medicine and Hypnosis at Gutenberg University, Mainz, West Germany, Dr. Banerjee boldly stated the following:

> ...I have attempted to show scientists and hypnotists who are using hypnosis to understand the nature of man that the scientific study of reincarnation is valid, an idea which is contrary to their usual opinion that reincarnation is a fantasy with no empirical evidence in its favor.
>
> This view is a prejudgment based on inappropriate data. In order to support this stand, I have, in general, discussed the problem of reincarnation and, in particular,

have explained in detail the empirical study of one case of reincarnation out of hundreds studied by me.

The case mentioned in this paper [that of an individual named Gopal] was carefully studied in a scientific manner, *i.e.* reincarnation was not blindly accepted, but rather all possible explanations and hypotheses were examined and weighed for their credibility. It seems that the case is suggestive of reincarnation. It should be mentioned here that when the study of the case of Gopal was completed, it was independently corroborated by the Department of Psychology, University of Delhi.

With the help of this paper, I wish to emphasize the following points so they may be considered.

1. The issue of reincarnation is still open. It should not be considered to be a fantasy or a religious myth.

2. Reincarnation should be viewed without prejudice. Studies should be conducted with the help of hypnosis in order to determine the element of prejudice, either for or against, in researchers studying reincarnation, *i.e.* scientists, hypnotists, etc., who pronounce judgment on reincarnation. This study would result in a much-needed, unbiased approach to reincarnation.

3. Reincarnation should be considered a special psychological process which possibly appears only in some persons, *e.g.* the phenomenon of prodigy. Therefore, selected cases which merit investigation should be studied.

Scarcity of cases should not be used as evidence against the phenomenon of reincarnation. For example, yellow fever is prevalent only in certain countries, but from this fact it cannot be concluded by the people of a country having no trace of yellow fever that there is no such thing as yellow fever. Efforts should be made to find out the psychological and sociological factors which limit the occurrence of reincarnation in some geographic regions, and which, in contrast, provide an ideal climate for it to appear more frequently in other regions.

4. Finally, I wish to appeal to scientists using hypnosis and hypnotists to join forces with parapsychologists who are trying to understand reincarnation. They could greatly help in the study of a reincarnation case by putting the subject under hypnosis to determine how far his claims of reincarnation are due to conscious or subconscious learning.

I, as a parapsychologist, am placing the Gopal case of reincarnation before the scrutiny of scientists and hypnotists so that they can reevaluate the problem in the light of fresh data.

1. Brad Steiger *You Will Live Again* (Dell Publishing and the Confucian Press, Inc., NY: 1978).

5

Receiving Help from Your Spiritual Guide

We have found that permitting an individual to meet his or her psychic guide or master teacher is an extremely effective way to move farther and faster with a subject.

Many men and women who attend our seminars already believe in—or at least are open to—the concept that benevolent multidimensional beings stand ready to guide and protect them while they are in an altered state of consciousness. Whether or not the theory of guides fits into anyone's prior cosmology is unimportant. It remains an excellent device for fostering feelings of security and for accelerating the process of exploring past lives, out-of-body experiences, and vision quests.

By now many readers will be familiar with the accounts of Francie's interaction with her angelic guide, Kihief. This multidimensional being has maintained contact with her since she was about the age of five. It is this being who has shaped many of the techniques and awareness exercises in this book.

Francie's ability to communicate with Kihief has been evaluated by Forrest L. Erickson, one of the nation's leading users of the Psychological Stress Evaluator, the P.S.E., a space-age lie detector.

The P.S.E. was developed by two colonels in military security; the device has the capability of analyzing a subject's voice patterns and of detecting certain stress-related tremors controlled by involuntary muscles triggered by the unconscious mind. The P.S.E. detects, measures, and records in a graphic manner any guilt-revealing variations in the human voice. It is currently being used by insurance investigators, police departments, and both military and civil courts.

For her test Francie told of her initial activating experience during childhood, when Kihief materialized before her. Next she went on to describe various circumstances under which she was later given teachings by the master. She was quizzed thoroughly about what she learned and about specific items relating to the material. When Forrest Erickson released his findings of the test, he stated that in every instance analyzed, Francie was totally innocent of any deception.

In a subsequent test Erickson testified that Francie's voice was free of the stress that would indicate untruthfulness when she told of meeting with her angelic guide and her teacher and of being taken to a timeless realm to be shown living diagrams and teaching visions.

The kind of experience and encounters with a guide that Francie enjoys is available for every sincere seeker of love, wisdom and knowledge. But again we stress, even if your personal beliefs permit you to consider such entities only as creations of your own psyche, the mechanism itself is extremely effective in guiding you back into what may be memories of former life experiences.

Meeting Your Guide

Here is a relaxation technique we have employed with great success. It will place you in a state of consciousness that will enable you to reach out to establish a linkup with your guide, your master teacher, or with a more aware aspect of yourself.

As we have previously instructed, it is possible for you to read this relaxation technique, pausing now and then to permit its effectiveness to permeate your essence. It is possible for you to read the techniques of contact, pausing now and then to contemplate the significance of your inner journey and to receive elevation to a higher state of consciousness.

It is also very helpful to read the techniques to another person or to have another person read these instructions to you.

And as we suggested, you might even wish to record your voice reading these exercises into a cassette and play the tape back, allowing your own voice to guide you through the techniques.

Any of these methods can be effective. Your success will depend upon your willingness to permit such an experience to manifest itself in your conscious mind.

Imagine that you are lying on a blanket on a beautiful stretch of beach. You are lying in the sun or in the shade, whichever you prefer.

You are listening to the sounds of Mother Ocean, the rhythmic sound of the waves as they lap against the shore. You are listening to the same restful lullaby that Mother Ocean has been singing to men and women for thousands and thousands of years.

As you relax, you know that nothing will disturb you, nothing will distress you, nothing will molest or bother you in any way. Even now you are becoming aware of a golden light of love, wisdom, and knowledge that is moving over you, protecting you.

You know that you have nothing to fear. Nothing can harm you.

As you listen to the sound of the ocean waves, you feel all tension leaving your body. The sound of the waves helps you to become more and more relaxed.

With every breath you take you find yourself feeling better. You must permit your body to relax so that you may rise to higher states of consciousness.

Your body must relax so that the Real You may rise higher and higher to greater states of awareness.

You are feeling a beautiful energy of tranquility, peace, and love entering your feet; and you feel every muscle in your feet relaxing.

That beautiful energy of tranquility, peace, and love moves up your legs, into your ankles, your calves, your knees, your thighs; and you feel every muscle in your ankles, your calves, your knees, your thighs relaxing, relaxing, relaxing.

If you should hear any sound at all—a slamming door, a honking horn, a shouting voice—that sound will not disturb you. That sound will help you to relax even more.

Nothing will disturb you. Nothing will distress you in any way.

And now that beautiful energy of tranquility, peace, and love is moving up to your hips, your stomach, your back; and you feel every muscle in your hips, your stomach, your back relaxing, relaxing, relaxing.

With every breath that you take you find that your body is becoming more and more relaxed.

Now the beautiful energy of tranquility, peace, and love enters your chest, your shoulders, your arms, even your fingers. And you feel every muscle in your chest, your shoulders, your arms, and your fingers relaxing, relaxing, relaxing.

And with every breath that you take you find that you are becoming more and more relaxed. Every part of your body is becoming free of tension.

Now that beautiful energy of tranquility, peace, and love moves into neck, your face, the very top of your head. And you feel every muscle in your neck, your face, and the very top of your head relaxing, relaxing, relaxing, relaxing.

Your body is now relaxing, but your mind—your True Self—is very aware.

And now a beautiful golden globe of light is moving toward you.

You are not afraid, for you realize, you *know*, that within this golden globe of light is your angel guide, your guardian angel who has loved you since *before* you became you.

Feel the love as this presence comes closer to you. Feel the vibrations of love moving over you—warm, peaceful, tranquil.

You know that within this golden globe of light is someone who has always loved you just as you are.

You have been aware of this loving, guiding presence ever since you were a child, a very small child.

You have been aware that this intelligence has always loved you... just as you are... no facades, no masks, no pretenses.

This intelligence has loved you with Heavenly love. It has never been, "I'll love you if you love me. . . I'll do this for you if you do this for me." No, this angel guide has loved you unconditionally, with Heavenly love, love that accepts you just as you are.

You feel that love moving all around you. And look! Two eyes are beginning to form in the midst of the golden light. The eyes of your angel guide. Feel the love flowing to you from your angel guide.

Now a face is forming. Oh, look at the smile on the lips of your angel guide. Feel the love that flows from your angel guide to you.

Now a body is forming. Behold the beauty of form, structure, and stature of your angel guide. *Feel* the love that flows to you from the very presence of your angel guide.

Your angel guide is now stretching forth a loving hand to you. Take that hand in yours. Lift up your hand and accept your angel guide's hand into yours. *Feel* the love flowing through you. *Feel* the love as you and your angel guide blend and flow together.

Now, hand in hand, you feel yourself being lifted higher

and higher. Your angel guide is taking you to that other dimension, that other dimension for which you have always longed. You are moving higher, higher, higher.

Colors and lights are moving past you . . . red, orange, yellow, green, blue, violet, gold, purple.

Stars seem to be moving around you. It seems as though you are moving through space. You are moving into another dimension of time and space.

You are moving into a higher vibration.

You are moving toward a place of higher awareness, of higher consciousness.

Now you have arrived in that place for which you have always yearned. Look around you. The trees, grass, sky, *everything* is more alive here. The colors are more vivid.

And look at you. You, too, have been transformed. It is as if you suddenly have a new nervous system, new eyes to see those things that you have never before seen . . . new ears to hear what you have never before heard.

You are clothed in a robe of your favorite color. Sandals are on your feet.

And look ahead—the beautiful crystal city. Sunbeams are reflecting from every tower, every spire, every turret.

You know where you are . . . you *remember*. You've come home to one of your true homes beyond the stars. You remember this place, this beautiful, spiritual place.

Look at the people coming to greet you. Look at their eyes. Feel the love. You recognize so many of them.

Some you remember from your time beyond the stars.

Others are dear ones from the Earth plane who have already come home.

They reach out to touch you, to embrace you, to kiss you. And you feel the love flowing all around you.

As you follow your angel guide through the crystal city, you feel love all around you. Love as you have never felt it on Earth. Love as you have yearned for love all of your life. And you feel it now, all around you.

As you walk through those beautiful streets, you know where you are going. You know that your angel guide is leading you to the beautiful golden temple of love, wisdom, and knowledge.

You remember the garden, the lovely garden where you spent so many hours talking with your master teacher, the lovely garden that surrounds the beautiful temple.

There is the garden ahead. See the trees heavy with fruit. See the incredible array of colorful flowers. Smell the air, sweet as spring honey.

There is the beautiful silver stream that runs at the foot of the nine golden steps that lead to the great door of the temple of love, wisdom, and knowledge.

There is the bench where you used to sit with your master teacher. You remember this place.

Now, taking your angel guide's hand, you begin to walk up the nine golden steps. Feel the steps beneath your sandals.

The great door opens and you step inside. You *do* remember the golden temple.

Look at the great tapestry that covers the wall to your left. This tapestry reminds you that you are but a single, though important, thread that runs throughout the great fabric of life.

Look at the altar! There must be a thousand little candles burning and glowing before the beautiful golden altar.

See your master teacher is coming to greet you! Look at his eyes as he sees you. Look at his smile. He is crying, weeping with happiness that you have returned...if only for a visit.

He opens his arms. Go to those arms, feel them close around you.

He is saying, "Oh, my little one. I know that life has not always been easy for you on Earth; but remember, you may always call upon my name for aid and comfort. And if you have forgotten my name in your Earthly confusion, my name is..."

And you clearly hear the name of your master teacher.

Your angel guide speaks up and says, "Yes, you may always call upon my name as well when you feel that you need guidance and protection. My name is . . ."

And you clearly hear the name of your angel guide.

You know that you may return to the crystal city, the golden temple, nightly if you wish it.

You may return to receive the beautiful reinforcement of this love vibration as often as you desire it or require it.

And you will remember, clearly, the names of your master teacher and your angel guide.

Finding Your Teacher

Practice either the breathing technique or any other altered state technique to place yourself in a state of receptivity.

See yourself walking up a mountain trail in the light of a full moon. The trail is easy to see in the moonlight, and you have no fear of falling.

You are approaching an ashram, a spiritual retreat, wherein lives a very old and wise teacher.

Take a moment now to experience fully your emotions as you walk up the mountain trail. Feel deeply, savor your expectations.

Look around at the environment of the teacher.

What plants grow near the trail?

What is there about the mountains that most captures your attention?

As you approach the retreat, what do you most notice about the houses and outlying buildings?

Is there a garden?

Do trees grow near the main building? Take a moment to impress the ashram on your mind.

The master teacher whom you are seeking is said to be

able to answer any questions put to him. You are pleased that you have received an invitation from this old wise man to visit his ashram and to ask him any question that troubles you.

Now you turn off the mountain trail and begin to walk up the path that leads to the front gate of the ashram.

Be aware of all things near the path.

Be aware of your inner thoughts and feelings.

As you enter the gate, you are able to see the dancing flames of a great open fire burning in the center of a courtyard. You are able to see a man dressed in robes sitting near the fire. You know that it is a wise man, the master teacher.

As you approach the fire, a student steps forward and places more wood upon the flames. As they flare higher, you're able to see clearly the master teacher.

Become totally aware of him.

See his clothes, his body, his face, his eyes, his mouth, the way he holds his hands.

He gestures to you that you should be seated.

A student hands you a cup of the master's favorite tea, and you savor it gratefully.

Taste the tea in your mouth. It is very special tea, exceedingly flavorful, marvelously spicy, yet mild, gentle to the palate.

The master nods to you, indicating that you may now ask a question that is important to you.

As you ask your question, notice how he responds to your words. See how carefully he listens. See how thoughtfully he considers your question.

Continue to observe him closely.

He may answer your question with a facial expression alone.

He may answer your question with a gesture of the hands or a shrug of the shoulders.

Or he may answer your question at some length with

cautiously selected words.

He might even show you something. Some object or symbol might appear in his hands.

What kind of reply does he give you?

What answer do you receive?

Be certain that you understand completely what he has said.

How do you feel about what he has said? Are you pleased with his answer?

How do you feel toward the master?

The wise one is indicating that you may ask another question if you so desire. If you wish, ask the master another question, once again carefully observing the manner in which he answers.

Be careful again that you completely understand what the master is telling you.

A student steps forward and indicates that you must leave. The time allotted for your audience has passed.

Before you leave, speak to the master, tell him anything that you want him to know.

Now, as you are saying good-bye, the old one reaches in his robe and brings forth a leather bag. He tells you that he has a very special gift to present to you. He wishes you to take the object with you.

He opens the leather bag and hands you the gift. Look at it. See what it is.

Tell the master how you feel about him and about his gift. Say good-bye, for now you must leave.

As you walk down the path to the mountain trail, your thoughts are on the master, his answers to your questions, and the special gift he presented to you.

Once you are outside the gate of the ashram, open your hands and look at your gift once again in the moonlight. Turn it over in your hands. Smell it. Feel it. Discover all you can about the gift.

Is there anything you notice that you overlooked when

the master gave you the gift?

What deep significance does this gift have for you?

Know that you have the ability to use this gift wisely and to its most positive advantage.

Now begin walking down the mountain trail, carrying your gift with you. Look at all things near the trail very carefully. Look at the mountains and all the things around you.

Be totally aware of your surroundings so that you will be able to find your way back to the master teacher whenever you want to visit him and gain from his wisdom.

And now, with the thoughts of the master forever in your memory, with the true value of the gift forever impressed in your awareness, begin to return to full consciousness.

6

Balance Yourself—Banish Negativity

You can banish the dark forces that may be influencing your life. The following process is designed to remove any destructive force or curse, to drive away evil, and to silence even the demonic voices of darkness. This technique can increase your level of awareness, raise your spiritual vibrations, strengthen your shield of protection, and fill your life with balance, love, harmony, and beauty.

We all understand the merits of positive thinking. Volumes have been written on the matter, yet rarely are we given a practical working tool to change our perspective and make it more positive. The many methods that are suggested to us are frequently laborious techniques that take months, years to effect a total change.

It is generally recognized that fear causes us to be negative. Negative thinking is an accompanying vibration of all fear. Worry, anxiety, tension, panic, frustration, and hostility are the results of negative thinking. Fear causes uncertainty, doubt, and timidity, preventing you from achieving what could have been yours.

Fear depresses its captive to such a degree that he or she may become truly ill. Worry and anxiety, which come from fear, can tire you so that your mind and body actually become impaired.

Fear is a strong force, one that wreaks havoc in the lives of all who permit it to rule. It is the open door to negativity.

The only effective method to combat fear consists of a process of altering your belief construct regarding it. Methods used by many doctors, psychologists, psychiatrists, philosophers, and ministers are all based on this one fact: the belief construct regarding fears must be changed.

Only you can begin the first and most important step, perhaps the only step necessary, in affecting a total positive change in your life. You will then be able to break long-established habits of being fearful, negative.

Confidence is something everyone must learn to build, to acquire. You must condition yourself to become truly confident, for no one is born that way. Everyone you know who is confident has acquired that attitude.

You have spent your entire life acquiring negative memories. All of us suffer from such painful thoughts. Whether embarrassing or unpleasant, we remember them and may tend to dwell on them, viewing and reviewing them, seeing if we should, or could, have handled a particular person or event in another way—so as not to be victimized. Viewing and reviewing such an event reinforces it. We thereby reinforce the images of that unpleasant incident, frequently magnifying it until it is deeply carved into our psyches.

By the time we reach adulthood we have accumulated a mental storehouse full of battle scars of our lives. Some people "review" their daily psychic injuries just before falling asleep. In doing so they peel back scar tissue and reopen their wounds, which amplifies their suffering.

The people guilty of this form of self-sabotage cite various excuses for such negativity. Some say they review their past painful scenes so they will never fall into such situations again. Others claim that by comparing the former attitude they feel brought about such a wound, they can see how much they've grown. Still others contend that the more they review the old hurt, the less sting it carries for them.

Perhaps you are guilty of any one or all three of the above rationalizations, but all are *negative;* all are self-destructive; none should ever be practiced.

To become positive, you must counter the negative input that you place in your mind. You must fill yourself with positive memories, positive images—images of moments when you achieved goals, received praise, and were highly successful in whatever you did.

View and review that particular scene of positive accomplishment until its memory is indelibly imprinted on your mind.

Play this mental game with yourself. Feed yourself positive memories, positive images, continuously. If you were complimented on a particular choice of clothing, view and review that moment, etching it deep in your mind. Let the complimentary phrase ring and re-ring in your ears. This is one of the ways by which you can combat negative thinking, a negative self-image.

Another way of taking a giant step toward banishing negativity is to review your past mistakes, your past embarrassments in a *new* light, a new perspective. Perhaps you may have been far too young to handle a responsibility given to you. Perhaps anyone, unprepared, would have handled the situation similarly.

Cursing yourself after the fact is a cruel form of self-punishment, a form of negative hindsight, a far harsher judgment of you than that of an impartial observer. Learn to be kind to yourself. Become your best friend. Give yourself the benefit of the doubt.

Give yourself the same break you would give another person. Be as understanding with yourself as you would be with others. *Dismiss* the negative images for good. Think of them no more. If they attempt to enter your mind, gently wipe the mental blackboard clean. Banish them! Whether you suffer from fear of death, rejection, illness, failure, or even fear of the unknown (free-floating anxiety), you can conquer such fears by positive programming.

If not attended to, all of the above listed fears leave you weak, in a state of despair, unable to cope with life. These passive emotions can easily be overcome by a stronger emotion, since strong emotions always win when pitted against weaker ones. An example of this phenomenon can be seen in the behavior of those people who have conquered their fears by the strong negative emotion of anger. They have permitted strong anger to help them cope with their fears, and they become angry whenever they face weaker fears. Since they are bombarded daily with situations that are potential threats to their safety, well-being, and general physical survival, their reliance on conquering all fears with anger may reduce them to living in a perpetual state of aggression, ready to attack any situation or person they encounter. The end result may be just as disastrous as the original fear, for those filled daily with anger will suffer mentally and physically, as well as spiritually, with hateful negativity. The field of medicine has recently accepted the fact that a person's state of mind bears heavily on the state of his or her health. All is connected: we are spirit, mind, and body.

The most immediate way of accomplishing the goal of becoming positive is to reprogram yourself while in an altered state of consciousness. When in such a state you are most impressionable. Your "guard" is not on duty. You will accept more positive input instead of searching for reasons why certain suggestions may not be valid. You will accept more positive programming when you are in a relaxed, receptive state of mind.

It is very important that you permit yourself to become totally relaxed before you delve into the depths of your soul to explore uncharted territory. For if there is any fear, negativity, or reluctance in your mind, you will find yourself unable to be truly receptive to the suggestions given in the following chapters. You will be unable to journey beyond the present into the past to discover the many adventures and rich experiences hidden from your conscious mind.

The first step in banishing fears and negativity and in bringing about a receptive, balanced frame of mind is to achieve a state of total relaxation. The following is one recommended method, but don't feel limited; use the relaxation technique that proves most effective for you. You may want to have a trusted friend or relative read the following exercise to you, or you may prefer to record it in your own voice on a cassette recorder; use that method which puts you in the most positive frame of mind and which permits you most completely to relax. The value of recording this exercise on a cassette tape is that you can replay it whenever the need arises. Soft background music will aid you in relaxing. However, if a tape recorder is not available to you or if you prefer the presence of someone with whom you feel relaxed, the end result will be the same.

Soothing Fingers of the Sun Relaxation Technique

Lie down; make yourself totally comfortable. Be certain that the clothing you have on permits you to breathe easily and to relax. Be certain you will not be disturbed. Tell all who might bother you that you will be engaged for an hour. Leave the phone off the hook or silence it in some way. These procedures are advised in all techniques. You are now ready to relax.

Imagine you are walking toward a soft, green countryside—a beautiful, tranquil place. You select a plush grassy area on which to lie down. You place a fluffy spread on the softest spot and you nestle down into it. You know this is a perfect place to rest, to find peace, to enjoy nature. It is so lovely, so peaceful.

Lie down; stretch out; take a nice deep breath and relax here in your grassy bed. The sound of a nearby bubbling brook adds to the beauty of this tranquil place. The trickling water lapping over the rocks will help lull you to sleep.

Small, exquisitely colored birds sing melodiously, flitting from tree to tree. The soft sounds they make are so peaceful, so relaxing.

As you lie down on your back gazing upward, you notice that the sky is the clearest blue, with fluffy white clouds spotting it now and then. Some of the clouds hang as if suspended.

It is so peaceful, so lovely, so wonderful. Relax; your body is gently falling asleep.

You are becoming more and more relaxed and you find yourself breathing deeper and deeper.

A fresh, comfortable, cool breeze makes breathing so easy; you find yourself breathing slowly and deeply. You are becoming so relaxed, so wonderfully and soothingly relaxed.

Your taut muscles expand—then gently relax. It is so peaceful, so wonderful.

The breeze carries the faint, sweet fragrance of lilacs, a spring garden with a bouquet of aromas. Your body responds to this place with a great desire to sleep. Your breathing now is deeper, slower, more measured. You are taking long, deep, relaxing breaths of air.

Your body begins to fall gently asleep. You are becoming more and more relaxed, and you find yourself breathing deeper and easier.

The soothing, gentle warmth of an afternoon sun feels like loving, warm fingers massaging the muscles of your body, soothing you and helping you to fall asleep.

You can feel the soft, warm sun gently caressing, soothing the muscles in your feet. Feel the muscles in your feet relax; the toes relax; the balls of your feet relax; the arches and the heels relax. So peaceful, so soothing.

The warm, relaxing, gently massaging fingers move

over all the muscles of your calves, relaxing, soothing all the muscles.

The liquid-like fingers move upward, relaxing, soothing with healing warmth, the muscles in your knees, working deeply into the joints. Continuing upward, the liquid-like, gentle fingers of the sun relax and warm the muscles of your thighs, and you feel them stretch out and relax as if in a soothing sigh. You are so peaceful, so soothingly relaxed.

The wonderful, gentle motion of the massaging fingers of the sun work so gently into the muscles of your hips, healing, warming, soothing, going deep into the joints, going deep into the lower abdomen, deep, deep into the lower part of your back. You feel soothed, relaxed, and your body is falling gently asleep.

The soothing warmth slides gently into your waist and moves up into your spine, soothing all the muscles of your back. You feel your back relax and fall gently asleep. The liquid-like fingers of the sun soothingly travel around to your stomach and chest, soothing, massaging, lulling you to sleep.

Now the liquid-like, soothing fingers of the sun travel down your arms to your fingertips—relaxing, soothing you, and helping your entire body to fall asleep.

The gentle warmth of the sun slides up your neck and goes deep into the tight neck muscles, relaxing them, soothing them, and permitting you to fall asleep.

Now the liquid-like fingers of the sun gently massage your scalp. So soothing, so wonderfully relaxed. Sliding over your face, your eyes, your cheeks, your mouth and going deep into your jaw muscles . . . relaxing all the muscles, releasing all tension, helping you to fall asleep.

Nothing will disturb you. Any sound will only serve to help take you deeper and deeper into a more beautiful sleep. Every sound that you hear will help you to drift deeper and deeper into a very peaceful sleep. Whether it be the sound of a passing car . . . a closing door . . . a cough . . . or someone's voice . . . any sound and every sound will help your body to go deeper and deeper asleep, while your mind remembers everything. Your body is asleep, but your mind is aware. You are now ready for a most beautiful, positive, and wondrous venture.

Banishing Negativity to Achieve Balance

You know and fully understand the depth of all you receive. You know you possess free will, the choice to vibrate at a higher or lower frequency.

The vibrations of love, wisdom, and knowledge are available to you. They are the three highest vibrations that exist, and when they enter your being, when you utilize them, when you put them into practice in your life, you will vibrate with them.

There are those who have rejected the giving, and thereby the receiving, of unconditional love. There are those who have rejected the giving, and thereby the receiving, of true wisdom. There are those who have rejected the giving, and thereby the receiving, of true knowledge. There also exists those who have consciously rejected all three of these, the highest vibrations. They cannot give love, wisdom, or knowledge; nor can they ever receive them. These people vibrate with a very low frequency and they are vulnerable to the lesser and lower vibrations of Earth, vibrations of chaos, negativity, depression, apathy, hatred, avarice, and contempt.

When these people experience the death of their flesh, their spirit continues to vibrate at that very low frequency. The spirit that occupies their physical bodies becomes trapped in an area of nonliving, nonexisting and loneliness. It is a torturous area, devoid of all living things, devoid of love, wisdom, and knowledge. These three vibrations are the highest and they will not be found in the lower vibrational world.

Those whose minds are vibrating at a low vibration, who do not try to proceed forward on the path of awareness, who do not practice unconditional love toward *all* living things, operate on the lowest vibrational level they are capable of within themselves. Therefore they are accessible only to the realm of lowest vibrations.

If ever you are drugged to the point of being out of control, you are at that time vibrating at a lower frequency within yourself; and you are in the *path* of the lower vibrations of negativity, depression, apathy, hatred, and contempt at large in the world and beyond.

It should be easily understood that the highest vibration is unconditional love for all living things, for then one can be said truly to love God, the Source. The Source is responsible for the existence of *all* living things, and all things will return to the Source from which they came. Therefore, you must learn to respect and to love *all* living things, so that you will vibrate with the highest vibration that exists throughout all the Universe and beyond. For the Source of all things is endowed with all positiveness, all wisdom, all knowledge, all love. The Source has provided us with divine justice for all, thereby giving all who live perfect balance.

The law of cause and effect rules this world of polarities—this is justice. God is the highest.

What, then, is considered the opposite of the highest? The lowest, who is called by many names—evil, Satan, negativity. If God, the Source, is all wisdom, then Satan is ignorance. If God is divine justice, then Satan, the opposite, is without justice. If God is balance, then Satan, or negativity, is imbalance, distortion, chaos. If God is positive, then the opposite is negative.

Evil or negativity should be realized as an imbalance, a chaotic, ignorant, mindless, negative energy or vibration. It is a destructive energy, the opposite of growth and productivity.

The energy of negativity operates at an abnormal rate

and becomes an insane, frenzied energy capable of much destruction.

When you are negative, depressed, and do not vibrate with unconditional love for all things, you place yourself "on target," right in the path of that chaotic, mindless, destructive vibration that comes from the world of lesser energies, lower frequencies.

Remember, all that exists vibrates at its own particular frequency, at its own energy level. All those given free will can thereby raise or lower their vibrational frequency. This is the true understanding of free will: it is the will to vibrate at the frequency you desire, higher or lower; humankind has that choice. This is what distinguishes us from the animals.

Healings are accomplished when a person's imbalanced vibration rate becomes normalized or returns to its proper frequency. Every organ within us, every part of us, vibrates at a particular frequency, thereby causing us as whole persons to vibrate at that particular frequency. Remember, according to the world's many bibles, evil must always be cast out before the victim can be healed. *Hope* closes the door to fear. Every living thing responds to positiveness. The higher up on the evolutionary scale it is found, the more it responds to positiveness, love.

Plants have been found to respond well to soothing, symphonic, ethereal-type music. Plants withdraw and can eventually die when they are subjected to harsh, abrasive music. Plants have been shown, under laboratory tests, to respond positively to the vibration of love and to show little or no growth at all when subjected to the lesser vibration of hate.

Thoughts are positive or negative. Many times we have been confused by our lessons born in sadness, yet they may have been the ones that brought us the most awareness. Many of us have felt a painful experience to be evil or negative; later we realize we have misjudged it due to our limited vision. We cannot always see the total picture, the growth in awareness from having experienced the painful event. Instead we often bear the emotional pain, shut our eyes to the possible growth, and deem the experience negative.

We can make great strides if we change our perspective on things. We actually grow by enduring and by seeing through to the end those experiences that superficially appear to be evil. With the passage of time, after emotions have cooled, or after gaining further awareness, we can view events with a much clearer and different perspective. What at first might have been regarded as a curse can more clearly be perceived as a blessing in disguise—a blessing that has permitted us to gain greatly in awareness, thus raising our vibrational frequency.

If we could view all of life from an eternal timeless realm, we would be able to see that our sorrows result from our inability to understand and to comprehend the *total* picture. As long as we are seeking truth and proceeding forward on the path of awareness toward the Source, no evil or negativity can truly befall us.

We all have at least one major event in our lives that we do not fully understand, that, perhaps, we feel was brought to us solely for an evil purpose. Perhaps we regard this experience as having been totally negative in content.

To put this evil event in perspective of the *total* picture, think of timelessness, eternity, and feel yourself floating into that timeless, eternal realm. Feel the eternal energy here.

Now, in this timeless domain imagine before you the event that deeply hurt you, that you feel you still do not understand. Think of the tragedy that you experienced, you still know not why.

Be it the death of a loved one, the sadness at a parting, a painful marriage, a divorce or a separation, see the event before you as you might view a motion picture. See before you the images, the people, the activity that caused you the most pain, that you felt was evil and that you still do not understand.

Now, fill yourself completely with the unconditional love vibration and feel this love for all living things. Feel the unconditional love without any judgment or conditions placed upon it.

Feel your body as it fills with unconditional love for all living things, and imagine yourself as a kettle complete with spout. The spout is where your heart is. Now, pour out that love—send love toward the projected image, toward the picture before you—and watch closely, think and listen as the images change; and begin to understand the purpose for its existence, the reason for it all . . . See it, know it, understand why it occurred. See and know the reason it happened, feel the growth inside you. See, know, understand . . . (pause approximately twenty-five seconds).

Feel within you the positive unconditional love vibration. Learn to recognize the feeling of this vibrational frequency. Know and learn the difference between the good, positive love vibration and the lesser, negative, evil, hate-filled vibration. *Feel* the difference between the two. Feel and know and remember all that you have come to learn.

Continued practice of meditation of this sort will enable you to program yourself with positive energy, with love energy. You will be able to lift the veil of darkness and ignorance and come into a higher enlightenment, into the light where all things can then be perceived—where you can see your path of awareness to the Source more clearly.

Prayer is speaking; meditation is listening, receiving. Spend fifteen to twenty quiet minutes every day to develop proper receptivity to teachings, understandings, and awareness. Continue to meditate on your unconditional love for all living things, on the image of yourself as a kettle of love. Pour out this love on all the Earth, throughout all the Heavens, several times a day before sleep comes. This act of love will permit you to vibrate with the highest vibration. You will no longer be in the pathway of negativity and evil.

No imbalance can tune into you, can disrupt you or negate you. No evil can ever befall you.

When you vibrate with the highest vibration of love for all, you resonate with the sound of the Heavens. All positive, beautiful learnings and awarenesses will then be given to you. This must be an act you practice, you feel, you live, you believe in, until it becomes you.

You will notice that when you give unconditional love it can never be depleted, for you receive it anew from above. You cannot fill yourself with love, then hold it, for it will not keep, it will stagnate and soon sour. Love must be given so that you may receive it afresh.

Feel now this unconditional love, nonjudgmental love, pouring into your body, pouring into your feet . . . your ankles . . . your legs, hips, stomach, chest and back . . . your arms . . . up your spine . . . your head and neck. You are filled to the crown of your head. You are vibrating, glowing with unconditional love.

Now imagine before you the Earth and every living thing upon it. Show loving respect for the *lifeforce*, for it comes from the Source. Pour out unconditional love over all the Earth, giving it to *all* living things. Now feel it again pour into you through your spout.

You are giving and receiving anew the unconditional love vibration. Feel the energy, the strength of the love vibration.

Practice this always and no negativity can ever befall you, can ever harm you, can ever hurt you—or even *find* you again. Give and receive love. Remember this always.

You are now returning, still feeling the unconditional love vibration tingling through you. Feel your body coming awake, aware, alive.

As you name your body parts, they and all connected to them will come awake. Your feet . . . legs . . . hips . . . stomach . . . back . . . chest . . . arms . . . hands . . . shoulders . . . neck . . . head . . . face. . . all of your senses, awaken. Awaken, and vibrate positively!

7

Exploring Other Places You've Lived Before

I shouldn't even be telling you this," John said as he approached us at one of our past-life seminars.

"I have a good business in a small town, and I am the scoutmaster for our local troop. If word got out that I believed, or thought I believed, in such a thing as reincarnation, I might suddenly be thought unreliable, my business would die, and people would start spreading rumors that I was a nut. I couldn't work with the Boy Scouts anymore!"

John's glimpse at the unknown came while he was on a camping trip with nine scouts. Their plan was to hike up to Indian Cave, camp there overnight, then return before dusk on the following day.

"Indian Cave is a local landmark," John explained. "It is in a beautiful location down by the river, so it makes an ideal spot at which to camp. Not too many people like to trek to the cave, because there are no roads leading to it, so that makes it remote enough to give the boys an illusion of really roughing it.

"The walls of the cave still bear the evidence of ancient campfires. The arrowheads and Indian artifacts have long since been picked up, but there are still some old cave paintings which the Indians made. Some people say the paintings are fake and that the Indians didn't really make them, but they look pretty genuine to me."

John led his group of Boy Scouts to the cave that day and set them to work building campfires and clearing ground for their sleeping bags and tents. Later enough of them caught trout in a nearby stream to supplement the provisions they had brought from home.

After the usual campfire songs and hair-raising assortment of "real" ghost stories, John told his young charges to turn in. He sat up for a while, smoking his pipe before the fire, until the boys were all asleep.

John crawled into his own sleeping bag. He remembers thinking about what a beautiful night it was when ". . . the weird part of all this begins.

"I suppose I could have been dreaming, but it all seems too real to have been a dream. I don't know if it was the power of suggestion, sleeping there next to that old cave or what, but I all of a sudden had this feeling that I had slept on that *same* ground a long time ago. Only then I had been an Indian.

"I remember sitting up and feeling strange. Like you sometimes feel when you wake up in a strange hotel room and you don't know where you are for a few minutes.

"I looked at my hands and bare arms and seemed satisfied that they were brown skinned instead of white. I got up and looked at my reflection in the moonlight on the water.

"I couldn't see all of my face, it was too dark, but I could see enough to know that it was a different face from the one I have now, yet I knew that *it* was my face, too. I could see that I had long, shoulder-length hair, and it looked like I had some kind of beadwork pattern across the chest of my shirt.

"I just had this kind of wonderful feeling that I had come back to a very familiar place where I had had a lot of happy memories . . . as an Indian. The whole dream or vision, or whatever it was, was filled with my doing just simple little things. I mean, it wasn't a big Sitting Bull versus General Custer type thing, and I guess that was what made it all seem so real.

"I especially remember walking into the cave and looking at the drawings on the wall. I seemed to hold a burning branch in my hand for light.

"I smiled and nodded my head. For the first time the drawings seemed to make sense to me. In fact, as I walked under the stars the whole world seemed to make sense to me. Like there really was a Divine Plan and a logic to the Universe.

"I don't know. Say it was just a dream if you want to, but it seemed so real to me that I just have to believe that I've been walking around on this earth in one form or another for a long, long time."

John, as we shall see, is not alone in his conviction that he has lived before and has been able to recall memories of past incarnations.

Mark is a bright college student from Chicago. A bespectacled business major, Mark is typical of today's hardworking, no-nonsense, college men.

Most college students have long since traded in their desire to look "somewhere over the rainbow" for a high-paying job. Materialism shapes their appraisal of "borderline" experience, and if they cannot touch, see, smell, or hear it, they will not believe it. Wonderment is reserved only for what has already been accepted by the scientific establishment.

Mark was a typical child of his time until he went abroad on a six-week summer study program. At the end of the trip he was to write a paper comparing the various economic systems of Europe with that of the United States.

The son of a well-to-do businessman, Mark's passion was the world of high finance. He had a limited range of interests beyond the future of the marketplace. In fact, it took a concentrated effort on the part of Mark's friends and the accompanying faculty adviser to talk the young man into a day of sightseeing in the historic German city while they were awaiting the arrival of another group of students from the States.

Mark made little effort to hide his boredom as the guide led the small group of tourists through one of the massive castles that had been reconditioned for sight-seeing. Then, in spite of himself, Mark began to take a keen interest in the German guide's recitation of the events of historical significance that had taken place in or near the castle.

He felt his breathing become deeper and quicker. There was something about the stone hallways, the armor on the walls, the paintings, the feeling of the rough floor beneath his feet that began to seem strangely familiar.

". . . and this passageway leads to a dead end," the guide was saying. "The hall ends at a wall of solid stone."

"Not so," Mark blurted out. And no one appeared more startled at his comment than he.

The guide stared at him as if one of the suits of armor had suddenly spoken. Seldom did anyone interrupt his tour lecture, and no one had ever stopped his recitation to argue. These rude Americans!

"What did you say, Mark?" the faculty adviser to the group of young economists asked.

"I—I said that the guide is wrong when he says that passageway leads to a dead end," Mark replied.

The German guide regarded the young American coolly. "So how is it that I am wrong?" he demanded of his questioner.

"Tell him, Mark," one of his friends laughed. "Ol' Mark, who nearly flunked European history, is now going to lecture on Rhine castles!"

Mark was blushing furiously. "What I say is true."

"Well then," the guide snapped, upholstering a flashlight, "let us walk down the passageway and see who is correct!"

"Mark," the faculty adviser sighed, glancing at his watch, "time is growing short and we have other places to see. Why don't you just apologize to the guide and let us continue?"

"No!" the guide said firmly. "This young man called me a liar, and I must prove to him that he is wrong!"

"I didn't call you a liar," Mark objected. "I only meant that you were mistaken in saying that the passageway leads to a wall of stone."

The guide turned on his heel. "Follow me then!"

After the guide had led the members of the group who had elected to follow him about sixty feet down the dark passageway, he played his flashlight beam triumphantly over a dark wall.

"Do you call that a wall?" he asked Mark. "Is that not a wall of solid stone?"

Mark leaned his hand against the damp surface of the stone. "No," he said, slowly shaking his head. "There is a room beyond. A small room, but it is a room nonetheless. This wall has been added at a relatively recent period of time."

A collective groan went up from Mark's fellow students.

Forget it, Mark," one advised him. "Leave it alone so we can get on with the tour."

"But he seems so certain," said a well-dressed Englishwoman who had followed the group down the dark passageway out of curiosity. "Isn't there some way you might check it for him?"

Deciding upon self-control as the best means of keeping his job, the guide showed his teeth in an official smile. "Today is Wednesday. The curator is in his office on the main floor today. Perhaps if the young man will speak to the curator he will be satisfied. Now, let the rest of us continue our tour!"

To the amazement of his classmates, Mark did not let the matter drop.

Two of them, together with their faculty adviser, left the main group of tourists and followed their determined friend to the curator's office.

The curator listened patiently to Mark's story, asking him occasionally to repeat certain phrases, because, as he explained, his [the curator's] "American was not as okay as it should be."

"You are quite mistaken, young friend," the historian said with a note of finality after Mark had completed his contention that a room existed beyond the stone wall that sealed off the ancient corridor.

"Can't you check it?" Mark asked. "I'm certain that you are wrong."

The curator arched a craggy eyebrow, then scowled. "What is it that makes you such an authority on this castle?" he wanted to know.

But by now Mark's fierce determination had become contagious. "You must have some old blueprints of the castle," the faculty adviser said. "Perhaps you can match them against Mark's story."

The curator broke his stony silence by suddenly reaching for a cardboard tube on a filing cabinet behind him. With the tip of his pipe he began pushing a rolled-up map through the cylinder. "Here is a blueprint made of the castle in 1896—"

"Oh, much too late," Mark said shaking his head. "This castle was built in the twelfth century."

"There simply aren't many blueprints lying about from the twelfth century," the curator said, resuming his scowl.

Mark reached for pen and paper, sketched a diagram of the room he insisted lay beyond the stone wall. After he had finished his drawing, he named a German book.

He smacked his lips after speaking the title, as if the Germanic words tasted strange on his tongue. Mark's friends knew that he spoke only an elementary German.

For the first time the curator seemed to hear the young American. His scowl deepened and his jaws clamped tightly on his pipestem. He repeated the name of the volume, then directed a question to Mark in German.

When Mark only stared back at him uncomprehendingly, the scholar shrugged and turned to his bookshelves.

A few moments later the curator was blowing dust off an ancient volume. Carefully he turned the crisp and yellowed pages. Then, with a grunt of surprise he set the book before the waiting Americans.

"It is as our young friend says," the curator admitted, indicating a diagram on a page of the open book. "Originally the passageway extended to this small room. See, his drawing matches exactly with the plan in this book."

"But how did you know, Mark?" the faculty adviser asked his student.

Mark has been trying to answer that question ever since.

Did he pick up a memory pattern that had somehow charged the stones of the old castle?

Had he clairvoyantly divined the location of the secret room? Or had he come across another copy of the ancient book at some earlier time, forgotten the incident, and stored away the knowledge of the hidden room in his subconscious?

If one does not accept any of these hypotheses, then one is confronted with the alternative Mark does not enjoy considering. One must believe that in some earlier existence, Mark walked the passageways of that ancient castle unhindered by the stone wall.

Perhaps the room the thick walls had hidden had been his own.

Mark's experience may be a bit more dramatic than any you have undergone, but if you have experienced a somewhat similar recall you can number yourself among thousands of other men and women who have felt an overpowering attraction to another time, another place.

Your own experience may have been a spontaneous one, a transient one in which you felt a sudden, fleeting identification with a place that you had never seen before. Or you may be among those men and women we have met who have a nearly obsessional interest in a battle, a building site, a bustling empire, or a bucolic scene from a place and period no longer extant in our linear perception of time.

Whatever your personal circumstances, it is likely that from time to time you, like every thinking human being, have felt as though you should have been born in some other era, some earlier time. Men may yearn for a time when life was more simple and direct, far less complex and complicated. Women may long for a time when men were more gallant and protective. Our imaginations often focus on faraway times and places as having been much more romantic, secure, adventurous, or peaceful than our own.

Past-life exercise #1: As an experiment in spontaneous past-life recall, lie or sit in a comfortable position and permit yourself to relax as completely as possible. Take a deep breath, hold it for the count of three, then slowly exhale. Repeat this breathing process three times.

Begin to reflect on such questions as the following:

In moments of reverie ever since I was a child, I have often thought of living in another time. What was that time?

In what country did I live?

What sex was I?

What was my physical appearance?

What work did I do?

How many brothers and sisters did I have?

Did I ever marry?

How many children did I have?

Were my life situations happy or unhappy?

What were my greatest conflicts?

What were my greatest triumphs?

How did I die?

What was the most important lesson that I gained from that lifetime?

Did anyone in my present-life experience come with me from that lifetime?

What lesson or work am I to attempt to complete in my present-life experience?

Past-life exercise #2: As a second experiment in spontaneous past-life exploration, try this interesting inner journey.

After making yourself as comfortable as possible and practicing the deep breathing technique, permit yourself to recall or to fantasize a past life as a member of the opposite sex. Reflect on such questions as the following:

In what period of time and in what country or place did you live?

Were you a male or female?

What type of work did you do or what kind of training did you receive?

Concentrate on that past body and become fully and totally aware of it. What parts of it feel truly different from your present body?

How did you feel about your body in that life?

Describe every aspect of your body. Realize how being a male (or a female) made your life different from what it is now. How did you feel about being a male (or female)?

How many brothers or sisters did you have? How did they react to you because of your sex?

Did you ever marry? Reflect on your sex role with your spouse in that time.

Were your life situations basically happy or unhappy? How much did your happiness or unhappiness hinge on your sex role?

How many children did you have? Examine your role as mother or father.

How did you die?

What was the most important lesson that you were to receive from that lifetime?

Did anyone in your present lifetime come with you from that life experience?

What lesson or work are you to attempt to complete in this present lifetime?

Past-life exercise #3: For your continued exploration of spontaneous past-life recall, try this third experiment.

Once again assume a completely comfortable sitting or lying position. Prepare yourself with the breathing exercise, then allow yourself to recall or to fantasize a past life as a member of another race, a person with a skin color different from the one you now have. Reflect on such questions as the following:

In what period of time and in what country or place did you live?

What was your sex?

What was your appearance like?

What type of work did you do or what type of training did you receive?

Concentrate fully on your skin color. How do you feel about having been this color?

How did you feel about having been that color during that past life?

In what ways were your life situations directly influenced by having had that color skin in your past life?

How many brothers and sisters did you have?

Were your life situations basically happy or unhappy? How much did your happiness or unhappiness depend upon the color of your skin?

How did you die?

What was the most important lesson that you gained from that lifetime?

Did anyone in your present-life experience come with you from that lifetime?

What related lesson or work could you attempt to complete in your present-life experience!

Scanning Detailed Scenes From Past Lifetimes And Places

Use one of the relaxation techniques previously described in this book or a favorite exercise of your own. Use a method that will enable you to truly quiet your body and expand your awareness as fully as possible.

Again, you may read the following aloud to yourself, pausing now and then to contemplate the importance of certain images; or you may enlist the aid of another to read the technique to you in a quiet and thoughtful voice. Or, as suggested earlier, you might wish to record this technique and serve as your own guide through this inner journey through time.

After you have placed your body in as deep a state of relaxation as possible, proceed with the following technique:

Your body is now relaxed, but you have the ability to scan past lives for times and places that have always attracted you.

You will see scenes that you need to know about for your good and your gaining.

You will have the ability to see scenes from the past that have greatly affected your present-life experience.

Visualize a purple mist moving up around you. It is the purple mist of time.

You know that you have the ability to see and to scan all of time.

You know that you have the ability to see countries and periods of time that attract you the most.

You are moving farther and farther back in time.

You are moving back in time in North America. And you are seeing this nation when only the red man lived here. You see scattered villages on riverbanks, tall grasses, buffalo, deer.

You are moving farther back in time. You are now scanning Europe in the Middle Ages, when those nations which are now Europe were only a series of small villages on riverbanks, protected by the lord and his knights.

Now you are seeing Ancient Rome, the eternal city. You stand there on a street corner watching the mighty legions returning with yet another victory for Caesar.

You can see Ancient Greece . . . Athens, Sparta, philosopher-kings, poet-warriors . . .

Ancient Egypt . . . the Nile, pyramids, the sphinx, mystery . . .

Ancient Peru . . . walled cities high in the Andes, high priests cloaked in the feathers of many birds . . .

Atlantis . . . a dying empire being swept under a violent sea . . .

Back and forth in time you go . . . back and forth in time you go. And you see scenes from . . . foreign cities in Africa populated by proud black men and women . . .

China before there was the Great Wall . . .

Wagon trains moving across the plains . . .

The French Revolution . . .

Viking longboats setting forth to scour the shores of Europe . . .

You have the ability to see all of time . . .

You have the ability to see all of time . . .

Now you are surrounded by a golden light and a feeling of being loved unconditionally by one who has always loved you just as you are.

You are sensing the presence of an intelligence that you have felt around you since you were a child.

Now that golden light begins to swirl into form and substance. You see the shape of a body . . . hair . . . a beautiful smile . . . And look at those eyes, *feel* the love, the unconditional love, the unconditional love flowing out of you from those eyes. And now, standing there before you, you see your guide.

Your guide's eyes are filled with love, and a firm but loving hand stretches forth to take your hand.

Feel the love flowing through you. Feel the love from one

who has always loved you just as you are. Loved you with pure, Heavenly, unconditional love.

Now the purple mist of time is moving up around you. You find yourself in a beautiful garden surrounding a majestic temple.

You are viewing a scene from a past life in which you devoted yourself to spiritual service. Oh, you remember this garden! And you remember in which country you lived during this life experience.

When the bell sounds, you will enter the beautiful temple.

See the bench over there beside the lovely stream? You remember that bench. You spent many hours there with a wise and loving teacher.

There's the bell! Now walk up the steps that lead to the temple. Now step inside.

Oh, remember the beauty of this place! See the altar bedecked with hundreds of candles. See the artwork on the walls.

Look who is coming to greet you! Your former teacher, your guru, who taught you many things. See the love in those eyes as your teacher sees you.

And now, looking deeply into those eyes, remember the *name* of your teacher.

And now, looking deeply into those eyes, see if that teacher has come with you in your present-life experience. See if you have come together again to complete a lesson left unlearned, to finish some work left undone.

Look into those eyes and you will know. For your good and your gaining, you will know.

The purple mist comes up around you again and you find yourself in a scene from another past-life experience.

You are witnessing yourself in a scene from a lifetime in which you had a deep and meaningful relationship with your parents. You know the time period. You know the country.

A man and a woman are approaching you now. Look

into those eyes. Feel the love from those eyes.

And now, looking deeply into those eyes, see if you have come together with that man and that woman again in your present-life experience.

For your good and your gaining see if you have come together again to complete a lesson left unlearned, to finish some work left undone.

Look at the eyes of the woman and you will know.

Look at the eyes of the man and you will know.

They may not have come this time as your parents, but as friends, teachers, relatives, business associates, or perhaps even your own children. But look into the eyes, and you will know. You will know if they are returned to complete a circle of love with you.

In that same lifetime you are watching another person coming toward you. It may be a man or it may be a woman. You are looking at the eyes, and you see that it is a brother or a sister from that same life experience.

It may be a brother or a sister with whom you had a deep and beautiful relationship.

It may be a brother or a sister with whom you had a conflict, a misunderstanding, a deep-seated quarrel.

But you are looking at the eyes and you will know. You will know if that brother or that sister has come into your life again to complete a lesson left unlearned, to finish some work left undone. Look at the eyes and you will know if that person has come with you to take a role in your present-life experience.

You are now seeing the purple mist coming up around you again, and you are now viewing a scene from a lifetime in which you had to struggle against great odds in order to achieve a meaningful goal.

Everything that you see will be for your good and your gaining.

Nothing will disturb you. Nothing will distress you.

You will be able to see everything from a detached and

unemotional point of view.

You may be seeing yourself in a work situation, a political situation; you may even be seeing yourself fighting in a war. You are seeing it for your good and your gaining. You are detached, unemotional. You are totally aware of the time and the country in which this great struggle occurred.

You are now seeing a friend or a loved one who supported you throughout your great struggle.

This is one who was always there, who never failed you. Look deep into the loving eyes of that one who always loved and supported you.

For your good and your gaining see if that friend, that loved one, came with you in your present-life experience, to complete a lesson left unlearned, to finish work left undone. Look into the eyes and you will know.

And now you are looking into the eyes of one who steadfastly opposed you in that lifetime.

This is one who tried to block everything you attempted. Look into those eyes, deep into those eyes, and for your good and your gaining see if that one who opposed you came with you in your present-life experience, to complete a lesson left unlearned, to finish work left undone. Look into the eyes and you will know.

Now you are moving through the purple mist of time to another past-life experience. You are moving to view a scene from a past life when you had very special abilities. Some may even have called you a witch, a wizard, a sorcerer.

See in what time period and in what country you learned these special abilities.

See *how* you acquired them.

See *from whom* you acquired these very special abilities.

Look deep into those eyes and for your good and your gaining see if that person has come with you in your present-life experience, to complete a lesson left unlearned, to finish work left undone.

And now, most importantly, see *how* you used your

special abilities. Did you use them for good...or in negative ways?

See clearly what special lesson you learned from that life experience.

An now a brilliant ray of sunlight shines through the purple mist of time and you find yourself in a past-life experience in which you had a powerful, beautiful love relationship. Know in what country you had this great love. Know in what time you had this magnificent relationship. See now as that person approaches you again. Feel the love coming from those eyes.

Feel the eyes of that beloved one upon you again. This is one who loved you so deeply, so intensely. This is one who was always there when you needed love and support, when you needed someone to hold you.

This is the one who was always there to dry your tears, to hold you close and whisper, "It's all right. Everything will be all right, as long as we are always together."

And now look deep into the eyes of that beloved one as you feel once again those wonderful arms move around you, those lips touch your own.

Look deeply into those eyes and for your good and your gaining see if that beloved one has come with you again, to complete a lesson left unlearned, to finish work left undone.

See if this beloved one has come to you again. See if you were born again to be together. See if you have come together again to complete a beautiful cycle of love.

Look into the eyes and you will know. Look into the eyes and you will know.

8
Reaping What You've Sown—The Lifetime that Most Affects You Now

Louise was in a distraught condition when we first encountered her. And understandably so. She was a married woman who had been deeply involved with Barry, who was also married, for nearly three years.

"Like the song says, it is so miserable to belong to someone else when the right person comes into your life." said Louise.

Louise had been an executive secretary with a top firm in New York when Barry joined the company as a junior executive. Although she was about to become the president's "girl Friday," she manipulated interoffice politics so that she could assume the position of Barry's secretary.

"I had never been drawn to a man like that in my entire life," Louise claimed. "There I was: thirty-two years old, married, with an eight-year-old son. And I soon learned that Barry was thirty-seven, married, with three kids. We weren't a couple of love-struck kids who suddenly go bananas over each other. But it was soon apparent that he was just as infatuated with me."

They had tried not to make their feelings toward one another too obvious, but soon caution no longer made sense to either of them.

"We were soon finding excuses to work late. Excuses that would seem reasonable to our respective mates, that is. On the first night alone in Barry's office, we really came on to each other. It wasn't long before we were all over each other. We just decided not to fight it any longer—even though we had only been working together for less than two months—and we left the office to check into a hotel."

How had Louise been able to justify her behavior?

"My relationship with my husband, Steve, had never been really super, and it had definitely been going downhill for the past few years. Barry was simply everything that I had ever wanted in a man. It was as if he were cut from some mold or pattern that I had etched into my brain. Steve was basically a good guy, and I knew that in some way I would always love him, but he just couldn't measure up to Barry."

And how had Barry dealt with the situation?

"Well, it was basically the same, really. Jeanette, his wife, was not a passionate woman, and Barry really needed a more responsive woman to handle his strong sex drive. I was really ready to do that for him. And Barry told me that I was his idea of what a woman should be. He told me he loved my looks, my brains, my figure, my sense of humor—everything."

If they had continued such an idyllic relationship for nearly three years, why hadn't they divorced their respective mates and married each other?

"That's the reason I have flown across the country to consult with you two. We've been reasonably discreet. Office rumormongers have had a great time with our relationship, but I don't think either Steve or Jeanette really knows for certain. We talk about getting divorces and getting married all the time, but neither of us seems to make the first move. In the meantime we've had a lot of stolen nights together and some fantastic weekends and trips when we've flown to some really neat places on company business. Can you imagine getting to conduct an affair in Honolulu,

San Francisco, Atlanta, Las Vegas, and San Juan, and all on an expense account?"

So perhaps it is all just fun and games and rationalizations?

"No, I didn't mean to make it sound that way, really. Barry and I worship the ground each other walks on. We idolize each other. Our only true happiness is when we are together."

And you really think that you two could keep such deep feelings for one another from Steve and Jeanette?

"Well, yes. I mean, we don't want to hurt them. We've been able to carry on our lives with them pretty much as before. Really, nothing has changed that much for Steve and Jeanette. What has changed is that Barry and I have found the most true and complete happiness of our lives!"

What, then, was Louise's purpose in coming to see us for a consultation?

"I've believed in reincarnation for as long as I can remember. I've read a lot of books on the subject. Barry is open to reincarnation, too. I want to see if we can find any clues about our love affair in a past life that we might have lived together."

We put on a cassette of forest sounds, complete with a gentle, soothing, musical brook. Louise sat quietly for a few moments, attuning herself to the tranquility that flowed around her. When we perceived that she had begun to calm herself, we used a technique of relaxation to bring her deep within herself.

Louise envisioned her guide as a bearded master teacher who sat waiting for her on a bench near a magnificent temple. We permitted them to have a meaningful dialogue, then we urged Louise to ask her guide to walk with her through the purple mist of time.

"Request of your guide," we suggested, "that he direct you to view a past-life experience that will shed some light on the dilemma you face with Barry."

Louise began to describe a woman with long black hair, large brown eyes, dressed in a simple dress of European country folks. Although Louise was light complexioned with blue eyes and soft brown hair in her present life, she was convinced that the woman she was seeing was herself as soul-expressed in that prior lifetime.

She began to weep at the sight of the man who approached her. The man was stout, rather roundfaced, but with kind, gentle eyes. Although it was not the slim, fashionable Barry in his three-piece business suit, Louise knew it was he.

As this life experience unfolded, Louise found herself living a simple, rustic existence in what appeared to be a rural area in France *circa* 1870. She and Barry had reared four kids, three of whom, fortunately for the parents, had been sons to help in the fields.

With unabashed delight Louise laughed as she described milking three fat cows every morning before breakfast. And in spite of an angry hen occasionally pecking at her hands, she appeared to take equal delight in gathering eggs.

It was an uneventful life. Louise told us of no scandals, no major tragedies, no great personal catastrophes. She and Barry had lived out their lives together in rural bliss.

Before we brought Louise back to full wakefulness, we asked her guide to show her scenes from other lifetimes she might have shared with Barry.

It soon became apparent that Louise and Barry had been together many times, for Louise was perceiving scenes of strife, passion, violence, warfare, and desperation. After she had viewed a representative number of prior situations, we suggested to Louise that she ask her master teacher for guidance in her relationship with Barry.

Louise leaned forward as if listening closely to a whispered message.

After a few moments of such interaction she began to weep. She was still crying softly as we brought her back to full consciousness.

"My guide told me that Barry and I had fulfilled our karmic debts to one another as we evolved through a series of past-life experiences," Louise told us, accepting a tissue from the box we always kept handy. "He . . . he said that in this lifetime . . . we must work out previous situations with others...with Steve and Jeanette."

It was obvious to us that Louise's past-life regression had borne very different fruit for her from that which she had expected.

"I think I was already beginning to suspect something like this," Louise admitted. "I think Barry might have been, too. I guess that is why, even though we were so happy together, we never got around to asking for divorces from Steve and Jeanette. Maybe we just came together again to kind of support each other for a while."

Louise discussed the situation with us. Painful as it might seem, she was resolved that Barry and she must now stay apart until they worked out their growth potential with Steve and Jeanette.

She left us with a smile. "Who knows?" she shrugged. "Maybe someday Barry and I will be together again. If not in this lifetime, then in another!"

From her earliest childhood Ethel had had a recurring dream. In this strange dream Ethel saw herself laughing in a raucous manner and swinging her body about in an abandoned and frenzied dance. She saw herself surrounded by the leaping flames of campfires. She heard the mounting tempo of clapping hands, the wild and sensous music rising to a climax of violent abandon. And always she was dancing, dancing like some unrestrained creature of pagan pleasures.

The most paradoxical aspect of Ethel's dream was that she was the daughter of a strict Baptist minister who considered any dance to be Satan's own jig.

When she was a child of eight, Ethel had been caught dancing in front of the radio by her father (a radio was permitted because of the news programs). She was spanked with the full force of her father's righteous indignation and forbidden ever to listen to those "infernal disc jockeys" again.

At age eleven Ethel had not yet learned to leave well enough alone. She came home from school one afternoon and asked her mother if she might take dancing lessons with two of her girl friends.

Her horrified mother duly reported the request to Ethel's father, who not only took her allowance away for two weeks but forbade her to continue her friendship with the two "dancing daughters of the Devil."

By the time she was a teenager Ethel had learned that dancing was only for young ladies who did not value their reputations; while her friends were having supervised record parties in the homes of "hedonistic parents," Ethel was sitting at home with a book from her father's approved reading list.

And yet in her dreams she would dance, dance, dance. And how glorious it was. Her hair was borne on the night wind like the mane of some marvelously spirited mare. She was barefoot. She could feel her feet striking the smooth earth with a rhythm that made her blood course hotly through her veins. And she would swirl her skirt—swirl and twist it high so that her flashing ankles and full thighs inflamed the desires of the cheering men. Mornings she would awaken feeling unclean and wonder why God permitted such obscene visions to torment her.

She considered confiding in her mother, but she knew that the story of the secret dream would soon find its way to her father's ears. She took no pleasure in the prospect that the Reverend might try to beat the Devil out of her.

"Life," Ethel wrote, "had settled into a rut of incredible frustration and torment. When I entered college and began to take some psychology courses, I theorized that my dream was a wish fulfillment. I was dreaming about dancing because I was not permitted by my parents to go to dances. I further observed that most girls my age did like to dance, and it was natural that I should have been so much in love with dancing even as a little girl."

Ethel had found the solution to the repetitive dream. Or so she believed.

It was at a New Year's Eve party that Ethel became more confused than ever. Ethel was a senior at the small church college she attended and would be graduating that June to become a social worker. Although she was regarded by all who knew her as an exceedingly prim and proper young woman, she was lovely and gracious enough never to lack boyfriends. Many young men were attracted but few passed the Reverend's extensive screening.

On this particular New Year's Eve the clergyman had been more intent on preparing the New Year's Eve Day sermon than in examining the moral credentials of the young man who had asked Ethel to accompany him to a "quiet, well-chaperoned party."

Charlie, who had graduated from high school with Ethel, was known to have stretched the truth occasionally, to drink beer, and, when he could get it, hard liquor. He had boasted to many of his contemporaries that he intended to "thaw out that preacher's daughter."

The party, in short, was not the quiet, sober little get-together that Charlie had talked of to the Reverend. It was a noisy, liquor-sopping, jam-packed blast!

Ethel had a few moments of inner panic, but she got a good grip on Charlie's arm and entered the party fully determined to enjoy herself. She was, after all, going on twenty-two.

Ethel did, however, make Charlie promise "not to try to get her to take a drink." This was one promise the Charlie kept. He did not have to tease, cajole, or shame her into drinking. The fruit punch looked innocent but was laced with enough vodka to quench the thirst of the entire Bolshoi Ballet.

By the time the partygoers had assembled to play "Amateur Hour," Ethel was feeling so uninhibited that she had actually laughed at one of Charlie's off-color stories.

"Amateur Hour," Charlie explained to the newcomers in the group, was an old and honored tradition among the young people who had been gathering for New Year's Eve since the parent-chaperoned pop and popcorn parties of junior high school days. According to the rules each guest at the party must perform for the group when called upon or be subject to a prank by the other partygoers.

The first guest called upon, a young woman, sang "God Bless America" in a high, crackling soprano. The second contestant earned a solid round of applause for his imitation of their old high school principal.

Ethel was relieved to note that the critical standards of the audience had been suitably blunted by large doses of liquor.

Although she felt a slight repugnance at the sight of all her old high school friends in varying stages of inebriation, she was grateful that they would not be in any condition to place high demands upon the performances of the contestants in the amateur hour. She was grateful, too, that she had her wits about her and was in complete control of the situation. She called for Charlie to bring her another cup of that delicious fruit punch.

By the time Ethel was called to the floor by the master of ceremonies, there was a wicked sparkle in her eyes. Ethel was known to have a fine choir voice, so a reasonably sober young man had already taken his place at the piano in anticipation of her wishing to sing for their entertainment.

Ethel shocked all assembled by announcing that she intended to dance.

Most of the young people in the room had known Ethel since grade school. They knew full well the position of her clergyman father on the evils of dancing.

If they were shocked at Ethel's announcement, they

were openmouthed and wide-eyed when, after she requested that her accompanist play some "wild gypsy music," she put on a demonstration of the most abandoned and exotic dancing that any of them had ever witnessed.

Her hair, worn sedately in a bun piled atop her head, was undone and allowed to flow in sleek, dark ripples down to her shoulders. Her shoes were kicked into a corner and, barefooted, she executed difficult dance steps with style and grace. She tipped her head and laughed at the almost hypnotic effect her twirling skirt was having on the men in the crowd.

On and on she danced until she collapsed into the arms of a very pale Charlie.

When Ethel regained her sense of the present, she refused to believe the reports her friends made of her performance. She remembered nothing that happened after she moved through the crowd to the piano. She recalled that she had intended to ask the accompanist if he knew the melody of a popular ballad so that she might sing, but beyond that moment she could recollect nothing.

"But you danced like a professional," one of her girl friends told her.

"Like a gypsy!" put in another.

As her friends described her dance, Ethel felt a strange little hollow being clawed away in the pit of her stomach.

They were describing her dream! They had seen her as she had been seeing herself in the secret dream that had been haunting her since childhood.

Since that night Ethel has often tried to recapture the grace and skill she displayed at the party. Her efforts, as described by her close friends, have been "clumsy and awkward."

Charlie confessed to her about the vodka in the punch, but Ethel has refused to become intoxicated in an attempt to re-create the wild experience of her dream.

She did receive an interesting letter from a girl friend

who attended another college. The friend, a very talented and agile dancer, attempt to reproduce the dance steps she had seen Ethel execute for one of her instructors, a Spaniard with a great interest in his country's folk music.

"He said that I was dancing a very old dance of the *gitana*, the gypsies of Spain," she wrote Ethel, "and he asked me wherever had I seen such a dance performed."

Do the psychology texts provide complete answers when they speak of repression and wish fulfillment? Or had Ethel been maintaining a lifelong communication with her Karmic Counterpart while she was in the dream state?

Mark could hardly look us in the eye when he came to consult with us about his problem. He told us that he loved his wife, Carol, and that he did not wish to hurt her in any way; but from time to time he became so enraged at her that he beat her severely.

"And she's been so incredibly patient, loving and understanding about all this," he said in a voice just barely above a whisper. "It just makes me feel all the more like a creep."

What generally provoked Mark to beat Carol?

"No special thing, you know. Hell, one time it can be over the meal not being hot enough. Another time it can be because I think she's nagging me about something."

Had Carol ever had to seek medical attention? Had the beatings ever been that bad?

"Oh, yes, God forgive me, but they have. And I don't think our family doctor is going to buy the 'fall down the stairs' routine again."

And Carol accepted this state of affairs?

"She is really a special kind of woman. Don't get me wrong, she doesn't like me to beat up on her. She's not on an S-and-M trip, you know. But she forgives me, and she tries to understand. I mean, we talk about it a lot."

From what point of view have they discussed it?

"Well, like we try to figure out what sets me off. What makes me lose my temper in such a violent way."

And they had come up with no clues whatsoever?

"Not really. Like I told you, it can be damn near anything. But there doesn't seem to be any pattern. It's not like I get mad every time she doesn't have the meal ready. It is never any one thing over and over."

We wanted to know if Mark had had a previous history of losing his temper to the point of violence.

"No, that's the weird, really weird, sad thing. I've never punched anyone out in my life. I've generally been a pussycat most of my life. Oh, sure, I used to get mad when I played football in high school, but I never carried it off the field. I have never had any fistfights at dances or anything like that."

Mark and Carol were a couple in their mid-twenties. They were tragically young to be mired in such dreadful domestic circumstances. As was often the case, they had already tried the usual round of marriage counselors, priests, psychologists, and other advisers without success. Carol had frankly labeled us the "last resort" when she called to make Mark's appointment.

We put on a cassette of sounds of ocean waves to establish a natural sound of relaxation. After Mark had attuned himself to the sound of Mother Sea, we began placing him in an altered state of consciousness through one of our relaxation techniques.

Although he had professed no formal religious training in our presession interview, his encounter with his guide, whom he saw as a guardian angel, proved to be extremely moving for him. We allowed Mark to savor his angelic interaction for several minutes, then we suggested that he ask his guardian angel to roll back the purple mist of time and permit him to see scenes from a past life that would illuminate the terrible passions that beset him in his present-life experience.

It was not long before Mark was reliving a time as a young Confederate soldier. It was during the closing days of the Civil War, and Mark was one of those rebels who chose not to surrender, but to carry on the conflict by becoming an outlaw. Together with Mark we relived a series of stage-coach holdups and armed robberies.

Then, as might be suspected, his luck ran out. He and two other men with him were ambushed by a sheriff's posse that had been sent to capture them. The two companions in crime were blown out of their saddles and Mark, too, had been hit. He survived his wounds, and in a trial that lasted a few seconds less than six minutes he was sentenced to a territorial prison.

It was at the prison that Mark ran afoul of a guard who had been a Union soldier. The man had lost his entire family to a renegade band made up of former Confederate soldiers, and he was convinced that Mark had been one of the murderers.

The guard began to hunt for ways to torment Mark. Before Mark's wounds had completely healed the guard had him working at hard labor on the rockpile. Once he decided that Mark had spat at his boot, and he had Mark placed in the sweatbox. Another time he had him flogged for dozing during the warden's reading of evening prayers.

On one occasion when the guard was beating Mark with his fists, Mark suddenly gasped: "My God! It's Carol! Carol is the guard beating me!"

We kept Mark unemotional, detached, but we continued to guide him through the terrible years at the territorial prison.

We learned that Mark was never released. The sadistic guard at last drove a pickaxe into his chest and killed him under the pretense that Mark had been trying to escape. With his dying breath we heard Mark vow to return from the grave and to make the guard pay for his brutalities.

As we guided Mark back to full wakefulness, we knew that we had one of those cases in which a victim had been reunited with his murderer in order to structure a positive expression of karma.

"How can such things be?" Mark wanted to know. "How could it be possible that Carol was that brutal guard? I mean, she wouldn't hurt a fly."

We explained that we could never fully understand how "such things could be," but we did say that it was obvious that Carol's soul, with its knowledge gained from other lifetimes, had been unable to reflect through the *persona* of the brutal, sadistic guard in that existence. In the present life Carol's soul was being compelled to interact with Mark in a positive manner so that the negativity of the prior existence might be balanced.

"Maybe that's why Carol has been so patient about all this," Mark told us. "Just maybe, on some level of consciousness, she remembers that life, too. Maybe she has kind of felt that I should punish her to help her atone for those sins, so to speak."

We thought that Mark could well have a point. Although we had observed that the working of karma could be subtle and intricate or pronounced and obvious, we did not hold with those who saw karma as punishment.

Karma is a compensation, a balance. Karma is a manifestation of the proverb that as we sow, so shall we reap. But karma is an act of balancing for the sake of soul evolution rather than punishment for the sake of misdeeds of the past.

"But I really believe that I have learned something valuable from this session with you two," Mark said. "There's been something so unreasonable about my beating Carol. It is so unlike the normal me to fly off the handle and release my temper in such a violent way.

"This past life that I relived today may be just farout enough to be true. At least it is something that I can focus on and think of whenever I feel myself losing control. I can remind myself that the reason for the anger happened in a previous lifetime to people who weren't really us, but facets of our souls."

Meeting The Karmic Counterpart

When we were working one-on-one with consultees in daily regression sessions, we found it exceedingly effective to focus on the particular past life that we came to call the Karmic Counterpart, that former existence which is directly responsible for the troublesome imbalance—the phobia, guilt, compulsion, illness, whatever—of the subject's present-life experience.

To assist our consultees we developed an elaborate three-hour session that blended a universal symbol system with anyone's personal cosmology. Although we can no longer provide personal consultations because of the press of writing commitments and seminars, we still wish to aid our fellow men and women on an individual basis. Several of the techniques we developed for those daily sessions are contained within the pages of this book. We have also committed that three-hour session to a cassette album, *The Starbirth Odyssey*, which we consider an excellent compromise in reaching a mass audience with individual attention. Projects such as this book and our cassette tapes are marvelous opportunities to touch hundreds of thousands of men and women with the energy and the love that we could formerly project only to one individual at a time.

We are convinced that a resolution with the Karmic Counterpart is essential to proper balance in the present-life experience. We have always been distressed to encounter men and women who had been tormented by their maladjusted lives, men and women who had been desperately consulting psychologists, psychiatrists, and medical doctors for years, with little or no progress made toward easing their pain.

Again and again in so many cases all we needed was one session with a subject in order to enable that person to see that he or she had been unknowingly permitting unconscious memories of a prior existence to ruin the chance of establishing a fruitful relationship or a productive life in the present-life experience. What was required was helping the consultee recognize the lessons that had left unlearned from that other time and to assist the person in using the proper mental tools to make his or her present life truly workable.

Here, now, is a technique to be utilized in meeting the Karmic Counterpart, so that an effective dialogue may be established between the prior self and the present self.

Use *any* of the relaxation procedures described in this book or utilize any technique that may have been successful for you in previous altered-states-of-consciousness exercises.

Once the body has been relaxed as deeply and completely as possible, permit the real you within the physical structure to become aware of a beautiful figure robed in violet standing near your sleeping body.

This beautiful figure is surrounded by an aura, a halo of golden light, and you know at once that you are beholding a guide who has come to take the *real you* out of your physical shell and to travel with you to a higher dimension where you will be able to receive knowledge of a past life that you need to know about, a past life that has greatly influenced your present-life experience.

This will be a past life in which you will probably see a good many men and women who have come with you in your present life . . . to complete a task left unfinished, to learn a lesson left unaccomplished.

Whatever you see, it will be for your good and your gaining, and your guide will be ever near, allowing nothing to harm you. Your guide will be ever ready to protect you.

Now you permit your guide to take you by your hand and to lift the *real you* out of your body.

Don't worry. Your spirit—the *real you*—will always return to your body, but for now you are free to soar, totally liberated of time and space.

The swirling purple mist is moving all around you; and

lifetime.

It is a brother or a sister with whom you had rivalry and conflict. Look at the *eyes*.

This is one who seemed to be undermining you in your relationship with your parents and with others.

Look into the eyes and see if you ever resolved your conflict with this person.

Look into the eyes and see if this brother or sister came with you in your present life in any way.

See if that brother or sister came with you to complete work left undone, a lesson left unrealized.

Now, back in that same lifetime, scan the vibration of any other relative or family member—an uncle, a grandparent, a cousin—and see if any relative or family member from that time has come with you in your present life . . . to complete a lesson left unlearned, work left undone.

In that same lifetime you are growing older, moving into young adulthood, and you see yourself performing some favorite activity, a game, a sport, a hobby, that became so much a part of your life *then* that it has, on one level of consciousness, affected your life today.

You see yourself performing that activity, and you understand how it has been impressed on the life pattern you exercise today.

You are now beginning to see clearly and to understand what work you did in that life . . . how you survived . . . how you provided for yourself or for others . . . how you spent your days.

Someone is approaching you from that work situation. Look into the eyes. This may have been someone who was your employer, your boss, your overseer. This may be someone who was your employee, your servant, your slave. But this is someone with whom you interacted closely at your work. For your good and your gaining look at the eyes, see if this person came with you in your present-life experience, to complete a work left undone, to learn a lesson left unaccomplished.

As you move away from your work situation, you are beginning to feel the vibrations of love moving all around you. You are aware of someone standing there, to your left, standing there in the shadows.

You are feeling love—warm, peaceful sensations of love—moving all around you, as you realize that standing there in the shadows is the person whom you loved most in that lifetime.

Look at the eyes. Feel the love flowing toward you from those beautiful eyes of your beloved.

Look at the smile of recognition on those lips as the beloved one sees you and begins to move toward you.

This is the one with whom you shared your most intimate moments—your hopes, your dreams, your moments of deepest love. And yes, your sorrows, your hurts, your moments of deepest pain.

This is the one who was always there—to love you, to support you, to take you in those beloved arms and say, "Don't worry. Everything is going to be all right. As long as we love each other and sustain each other, no one will ever be able to destroy us."

This is the one who always cared, who always loved and supported you.

Go to those arms again. Feel those beloved arms around you. Feel those lips on yours again.

Now, for your good and your gaining, looking at the eyes, see if this beloved one came with you in your present-life experience.

See if your love, like a golden cord, has stretched across time, space, generations, years, to entwine you again in the same beautiful love vibrations. See if you were born again to be together. See if you have come together again to work out a task left incomplete, a lesson left unlearned.

You are growing older in that life. See now the one whom you married in that life. Was it the one you loved most? Or was that beloved one taken from you by death...or by circumstances?

If the one you see before you now was not the one you loved most, then looking at the eyes, see for your good and your gaining the person you *did* marry. And see for your good and your gaining if that person came with you in your present life...to complete work left undone, a lesson left unlearned.

If you had children in that life, see them now. See their eyes looking up at you. Feel their little hands on your fingers. Feel the love flowing from them.

Did they grow older with you? Or were they taken from you by death or by circumstances?

Look at their eyes and for your good and your gaining see if any of those children came with you in your present-life experience to complete a lesson left unlearned, to be with you again in your love vibration.

Now see scenes from that life that you need to remember for your proper soul evolution.

See scenes that will trigger memories that will help you in your present-life experience.

See scenes that will show you clearly how certain patterns were formed then that have intruded, both positively and negatively, into your present-life experience.

These are scenes you need to remember, but you will see them in a detached manner. You will feel neither guilt nor shame. You will feel neither pride nor ego pleasure.

You will understand them—*why* they happened. You will understand these acts so that your soul may grow and gain.

The first scene you are viewing is a negative one. It is a scene in which you did something that has negatively influenced your present-life experience.

It may be a scene of violence, greed, lust, theft, brutality—murder; but you are observing it now and you are understanding *why* you did this act.

The second scene you are viewing is a positive one. It is a scene in which you did something that has positively influenced your present-life experience.

It may be a scene of charity, kindness, love, self-sacrifice, martyrdom; but you are observing it now and you are understanding *why* you did this act.

And now, for your good and your gaining, witness the moment of your death in *that* life.

Perhaps you weren't ready for death . . . perhaps you fought against it . . . cursed it. But understand *why* your soul withdrew its energy at that time.

See who was with you at that last moment. Was the one you loved most there? Your family? Your children? Or . . . were you all alone? Did you face that last moment alone?

See your spirit rising from its physical shell. See yourself being met by your very own angel guide, the same guide who is with you from lifetime to lifetime.

With a flash of insight your angel guide is showing you *why* you lived that life and why you lived it with those with whom you did.

You see clearly *why* you had to come again to put on the fleshly clothes of Earth.

You see *why* you had to come in your present life as the person you are now.

You see *why* certain people from that life have come with you again . . . to complete work left undone, to master a lesson left unlearned.

In another flash of insight you are seeing and understanding *why* you came to Earth for the very first time.

You are remembering *why* you chose to put on the karmic vibrations of Earth and come to this planet for the very first time. You are remembering clearly *why* you came here. You are remembering your true mission in life.

You see and understand clearly what you are to do in your present life that will most aid you to accomplish your mission.

You are filled with a wonderful sense of well-being, for now you know what you must do. You see clearly what you *must* do to fulfill totally your true mission in life. You no longer feel sensations of frustration and anxiety.

Now you *know*. You know why you came to Earth, why you chose to put on the clothes of Earth, why you chose to assume the karmic vibrations of this planet.

You are beginning to awaken, feeling very, very good...very, very positive.

You are filled with a beautiful, glowing sense of your mission.

You are filled with the positive knowledge that you will be able to accomplish so much more good and gaining toward your true mission now that you are filled with awareness of your Karmic Counterpart.

Now you understand how that lifetime has been affecting your present life.

Now you understand so very much more of the great pattern of your lifetimes.

And you know that your guide will aid you, will assist you in completing your mission, in accomplishing what you truly came here to do.

Awaken filled with positive feelings of love, wisdom, and knowledge. Awaken feeling very, very good in the body, mind, and spirit. Awaken feeling better than you have felt in weeks, in months, in years. Awaken filled with love, filled with wisdom, filled with knowledge.

9

Saying Good-Bye to Your Guilt

Millie had large dark circles under her eyes as she sobbed out her story to us.

"I must tell you that I am considering divorcing Clark," she said between sobs. "He has become obsessed with his work to the point of almost totally neglecting me and our children."

Millie told us that they had three children, ages seventeen, fifteen, and eleven, and that Clark isolated himself at work more and more with the birth of each child.

"Clark has always been a serious man," Millie informed us. "That was one of the things that attracted me to him when we were dating in college. He wasn't like some of the other fellows, who seemed only interested in drinking, playing cards, and fooling around. Clark supported himself with a part-time job and worked hard at his studies."

We pointed out that any responsible man might feel the financial burden of three children, especially as two of them approached college age.

Millie conceded this, but she added, "There is no need for Clark to be such a workaholic. He makes very good money, and until a few years ago I worked full-time and put nearly all of my income into our savings. Right now we have set aside nearly enough to put the kids through college—unless they all want to be doctors or something."

Millie said that even her assurances that she would go back to work, at least part-time, had done nothing to appease Clark's obsession with earning more and more money.

I'm afraid that earning money for the sake of earning money has got hold of Clark," she said sadly. "And it's not that he's become obsessed by possessions. If anything, he is almost a miser."

Millie went on to say that things had become so bad that Clark had taken to working through the children's birthday parties. "Begrudgingly, he takes time off for the family meal at Christmas and Thanksgiving," she sighed. "But we all know that he will probably go back to the office for at least a few hours sometime during the afternoon."

Her eyes brimmed with tears. "Really," she told us with a quivering voice, "I don't think I can take this marriage any longer."

We used a technique of relaxation to bring Millie deep within herself, then brought her into meaningful contact with her otherworldy guide.

We asked her guide to permit Millie to view herself in a past-life situation she might have shared with Clark.

We asked that she be able to see a past-life experience in which, whether she had lived with Clark or with another, she would clearly see herself in a past life to better understand the torment that so disturbed her in her present life.

Almost at once Millie was viewing herself tending to a large family in a crude hut. She was married to an earlier expression of the soul that now lived as Clark and they were living in terrible poverty. They were struggling to survive in a land that was blighted by a famine.

Through Millie's inner eyes we saw Clark tilling the soil, desperately attempting to wrest a living from the land. We saw how valiantly this man was seeking to provide sustenance for his family.

As Millie moved through that lifetime, we stood beside her and Clark when they buried five of their eight children, as one by one they starved to death. Together with Millie we heard Clark's tormented cry of self-condemnation as he cursed himself for having been a poor provider. We heard his tormented vow as he swore that he would work himself to the bone, if need be, so that the three remaining children would not perish.

Before we returned with Millie to the present-life experience we guided her through the remembered anguish to see all but one of the children died of starvation. We were, of course, careful to keep her as detached and as emotionally removed as possible.

We saw the entity that was now Clark collapsing of overwork and malnutrition and dying beside their infant son.

We saw Millie live to be a bent, pain-wracked, and embittered old woman who died alone and unmourned, deserted long before by a daughter who had had the good fortune to marry a man who was emigrating to the New World.

"My God," Millie gasped as she emerged from the altered state of consciousness with her new awareness. "What a terrible, terrible lifetime that was!"

She shook her head slowly. "Poor Clark. No wonder he has become so obsessed with providing for those kids. You know," she pondered aloud, "he wasn't a 'workaholic' when we were first married, but he became worse after the birth of each of the children. He was remembering, wasn't he?"

We agreed that it would appear that Clark's psyche had tapped into a soul memory of a lifetime when his children had died of starvation, regardless of how desperately he had worked to prevent it. Somehow the soul memory had filled Clark with a sense of guilt over the deaths of those poor children, and on a subconscious level he had been driven to see that such circumstances would not be duplicated in his present-life experience.

"I'm going to do everything that I can to help alleviate that sense of guilt," Millie resolved. "I'm going to tell Clark about our session and try to explain to him that the terrible thing he is trying so desperately to avoid has already taken place in a previous lifetime. Somehow, I'm going to get him to relax more and to enjoy life before he works himself into an early grave."

We suggested that Clark practice a series of meditations we sent with Millie, and we also provided a tape cassette that would enable him to explore his own past-life memories.

Many of us at some time or another in our lives are beset by vague or pronounced feelings of guilt. In these periods of anguish we may analyze why we have these gnawing sensations of remorse and shame. Try as we might, we can determine nothing in our present-life experience that should account for such guilty feelings. It is in such instances that we may wish to explore the possibility that our guilt originated in a past-life experience. Surely one has nothing to lose by attempting to ferret out the reason for one's discomfort in what may be a prior-life situation.

To reach into the past, lie or sit in a comfortable position and allow yourself to relax as totally as possible. Take a deep breath, hold it for the count of three, then slowly exhale. Repeat this breathing procedure three times.

Reflect on your guilt. Recall as completely as you can the emotions that flow through you when this feeling of guilt impinges upon your life. Recall as totally as you can the physical reactions your body undergoes when you experience this guilt that troubles you.

Now remember a recent situation in which you experienced these guilty feelings. Allow yourself to flow back into that situation and try to see it in your mind's eye as if it were happening at the present moment.

What first triggered the guilty response? Was it a word, a gesture, an attitude? Or was it your *response* to a word, a gesture, an attitude?

After the first tremor of guilt, what was said or done to make the feeling increase?

Was there a particular place in your body where you experienced physical tension or discomfort? Did you, for example, feel nausea, dizziness, trembling?

If so, reflect for a moment on precisely what part of your body reacted most to the guilt.

With this analysis in your mind reflect on what person in all the world you would least like to be aware of your guilt. Or which person in all the world you would least like to inform of your guilt. Focus now on that person. Project how this person would react if he or she found out about your guilt. Visualize that person's facial expressions. Visualize that person's physical reactions. Imagine what that person would say to you.

Now, focusing even more sharply on that person, fantasize that individual looking perhaps somewhat different from his or her present physical appearance. Imagine that person wearing clothing from some other historical era.

Continuing with the fantasy, project yourself to that same historical period. Perhaps you, too, are somewhat different in physical appearance.

Now imagine that you are involved with that person in a very unique way. Fantasize the particular relationship you had with that individual in that lifetime. Permit the fantasy to play itself out. See yourself making a commitment to this individual, stating a promise or, perhaps, making a vow. Now see why you did not fulfill your promised action.

Did you violate your commitment because of selfish or egotistical reasons? Or were you somehow blocked or prevented from making good your promise?

Tune in completely on the reason why you did not fulfill your intended action. Visualize the scene that left you with such a powerful residue of guilt that your soul's present expression is still suffering from the negative vibrations.

Now fantasize yourself explaining to the injured party, both as he or she appears in this lifetime and in the prior-life experience. Imagine an overlap of your personalities as you make your apology, as you state your case.

After you have made as fervent an explanation as possible, hear the injured party accept your apology and tell you that everything will now be fine between you.

Hear that individual associated with your feelings of guilt say that you have now completed the lesson you came together again to learn, that you have now accomplished the work you had left incomplete.

Let warm waves of unconditional love wash over your body. Know that on the soul level you have been forgiven. You need not feel that guilt ever again.

10

Freedom from Your Phobias

Brad knows about phobia from firsthand experience. He knows about the stomach-wrenching, heart-thudding, head-dizzying, unreasoning fear that can seize the body and brain at awkward moments. He used to have a terrible fear of flying that severely hampered his professional life until he had a profound past-life vision that instantly eliminated the fear.

For as long as Brad can remember he suffered a nightmare of being high in the air, being suddenly engulfed in a blast of noise and flame, then being hurtled through space. When he became old enough to attempt to understand his inner experiences, he became convinced that he would one day die in an aircraft explosion. As a child, he vowed to avoid air travel and thereby avoid his fate.

Flying was really not a problem early in his life. Automobile trips sufficed to get him wherever he wanted to go. But he had written a number of successful books, and the publishers' publicity people now were insisting that he make promotional trips.

In order to satisfy the demands for personal appearances Brad had to come to painful grips with his fear of flying. He had begun to drive the publicity people wild by forcing them to arrange promotional tours without the use of airplanes. He had to hop around the country by means of commuter trains, buses, and automobiles.

After a particularly dismal travel experience, Brad would resolve to fly. But then as he approached an air terminal, the gut-wrenching, sweat-popping fear of flying would force him to cancel the flight plans and seek a route to the next talk show by bus or train.

Today Brad logs several thousand miles of air travel each year. The "cure" of his fear of flying cannot be attributed to years of psychoanalysis, encounter groups, or any in-vogue therapy session. Brad's fear of flying was conquered by the catharsis of his psyche's undergoing the death experience in what would appear to be a profound vision of a past life.

Brad awakened one night (he is certain he was not dreaming) to view, as in a panoramic cinemascope movie, scenes from a world that appeared to have the flavor of northern Europe, specifically Germany, at the turn of the century.

He watched in wonder as he saw a life unfolding before his eyes. It was the life of an attorney in Bremen, Germany, a man who found himself embroiled in a great personal tragedy.

Interestingly Brad saw "himself" only when he would pass in front of a mirror or some other reflective surface. At all other times he was literally seeing the ensuing events through the eyes of the participant—who he "felt" was somehow an expression of the same soul that today manifests as Brad Steiger.

Because of the turmoil that surged uncontrollably around him, the attorney fled the city. He wandered throughout Europe for a number of years, studying, painting, writing. Then at the outbreak of World War I he enlisted in the German air force. The man lived for the moment, trying desperately to find meaning in his life by taking the lives of the enemies of his country.

Then on an especially sunny afternoon, high above the skies over France, he and his squadron mates encountered a group of British aircraft. While he was diving after his chosen prey, he became aware of a stinging in his shoulder. He looked around to see blood spurting. A British aircraft with twin machine guns was swooping right on his tail.

There was an explosion, a violent burst of flame, and he was aware of falling unsupported through space.

Stunned, Brad became once again aware of present-day reality around him. Then he realized that he had just witnessed an enactment of the events leading up to the nightmare that had troubled him ever since he was a small boy. He had just seen the full scope of the terrible dream that had placed him high in the air, had engulfed him in a blast of noise and flame, and had hurtled his body out into space.

Could it be possible, Brad asked himself, that he had actually once lived in Germany at the turn of the century, that he had been killed in aerial combat in World War I? Or had his creative psyche only fabricated a marvelously detailed psychodrama to provide him with a catharsis whereby he might travel by air and achieve a much more effective schedule for conducting research, giving lectures, and fulfilling promotional activities?

The really important thing about the apparent past-life vision was that it gave a new interpretation to Brad's lifelong sporadic dream. He was not fated to die in a midair explosion in this life. He had *already* died in such an explosion in a previous lifetime.

From Brad's perspective it is not important to him to prove whether or not that German pilot who died in a fiery midair explosion over the war-torn fields of France was truly a prior aspect of his soul. Brad is aware that his present self loathes war. He seeks in his work to help men and women realize that they have the potential to transcend the primitive impulses that lead to inhumanity, bloodshed, and the desecration of the sacred bond that should unite all people as brothers and sisters.

Brad is open to the theory that his memory-vision may have been the result of his own psyche's somehow attuning itself to the life pattern of someone else, someone who actually lived as an attorney in Bremen, Germany, prior to World War I.

Another possibility is that in an altered state of consciousness Brad managed in some manner to "plug" into a memory pattern that blended with his own psyche long enough to make it seem as though Brad himself had had those experiences in another lifetime.

Or as already suggested, a creative facet of Brad's psyche may have provided him with a framework whereby he could remove his fear of flying through an ingenious and extensively detailed interior psychodrama.

Whatever the eternal truth of Brad's experience may be, the important thing is that the vision served a most practical purpose. Because of that one burst of creativity or past-life memory, a fear that had crippled Brad since childhood was removed. Since that ostensible past-life recall he can now manage to sit near the window in a tall building. He can now walk up an open flight of stairs.

Because of that one revelatory vision Brad's fear of flying was removed, and he has never had a single repetition of those terrible falling dreams. Brad suffered no more white-knuckle flights, no more cold sweats, no nervous starts at every whir and thump of the aircraft. Brad can relax on board a plane to the point of deep and restful sleep. In all honesty he can now say that he enjoys flying.

Whatever Brad's past-life memory might be to you, it cannot simply be relegated to ethereal, impractical mysticism. Whatever else it may have been, Brad's vision was intensely practical and productive.

Throughout the many years of our research we have encountered many men and women who have suffered phobias because of a very negative past-life experience. Most often, it seems, these fears are associated with the death experience, as was Brad's. Although we would never presume to attempt to work with someone who had obvious and serious emotional problems, we found again and again that past-life exploration could often offer almost instantaneous solutions to phobias that had afflicted some of our subjects for several years.

Many of us at some time or other are troubled by phobic, fearful reactions to specific things or situations in our lives. Under certain conditions these fears have become so powerful that they have inhibited or restricted our lives severely. In some instances these phobias may have crippled us and prevented us from complete development of ourselves or from achieving total fulfillment as sovereign entities.

If we cannot determine from self-analysis of our present lives just why such fear has come into being, it may be useful to examine the possibility that the origin of the phobia lies in some prior existence. Although such memories may have become blocked from full realization by the survival mechanism of the present memory, they often may be brought into more complete consciousness by utilizing the following altered state technique.

Lie or sit comfortably in a position you can maintain without stress for a reasonably long period of time. Permit yourself to relax as completely as possible. Use one of the techniques of relaxation we have described in this book or a favorite method of your own.

Contemplate your fear.

Recall as totally as you can the emotions and physical responses that flow through you and constrict your brain and body.

Recall as completely as you can the quickening of the heart, the increase of the breath, the onset of heavy perspiration.

Remember a recent situation in which you experienced

a confrontation with your phobia. Go back to that situation. Try to see it in your mind's eye as precisely as if it were happening at the present moment.

Try to recall what it was that first triggered your phobic response.

Was it someone discussing a situation in which you would have to confront your fear?

Was it merely a reference to the subject matter of your fear?

Or did you actually confront the fear itself?

After you felt the first tremor of fear what did you do to make the feeling increase?

If there were others present, what did they do to make your fear increase?

Was there a particular place in your body where you actually seemed to feel the tension of fear more than any other?

Do you react most by trembling, feeling dizzy, or by feeling nauseous?

Reflect for a moment on exactly which part of your body reacted most to the phobia.

As you are reflecting on your body in such a manner, try to focus on why you respond more in that part of your physical structure than in any other.

Begin to fantasize in a free-associative manner. Did something connected with your fear once become localized in that part of your body? Did something strike you there? Burn you there? Bite you there? Crush you there?

Continue to free-associate in such a manner. Where were you when the incident occurred! See yourself in that environment. See yourself suffering the original trauma, whatever it may have been.

Now imagine that you can see clearly the historical period in which this trauma occurred. See yourself as you appeared at that time. See yourself wearing clothing from this earlier era.

See other people with whom you might have been intimately involved in that prior-life experience. Specifically see anyone who might have come with you in your present-life experience.

Focus again on the exact time reference of the original trauma. See if you survived the original traumatic act.

You will be detached and feel no strong emotional tie to the earlier expression of your soul. You will observe the event only for the purpose of freeing yourself from the fear that inhibits you today. You will observe the trauma only for the purpose of impressing upon all levels of your consciousness that the reason for the terrible fear that restricts you so in your present life is a thing of the past.

The phobia that so tortures you is the memory of an event that has *already* occurred. You will know and understand that the trauma has already been endured, already been spent, already been resolved, all in your very own existence.

Impress on all levels of your consciousness, all aspects of your awareness, that your feelings of crippling fear toward this object, this situation, this occurrence are unnecessary.

Impress on all levels of your consciousness, all aspects of your awareness, that you need not ever experience that fear again.

Impress on all levels of your consciousness, all aspects of your awareness, that the fear is dead. Understand that the fear and all its consequences were the stuff of another life experience. They constitute a memory that can now be forgotten. *Forgotten and dispensed with forever!*

11

Conquering Your Compulsions

A tearful woman named Katherine told us she knew that she was ruining her son's life but that she could not help herself. She had meddled in his relationships with the opposite sex ever since he had been a teenager.

By the time her son turned thirty she had been responsible for terminating two engagements, and she admitted to having been the direct cause of his divorce. To make matters worse, she confessed, she had sabotaged his dream of entering medical school.

"My husband has become so thoroughly disgusted with my behavior that he has threatened me with divorce," she said. "My son, Philip, has not spoken to me—I mean *really* spoken to me—since his marriage collapsed two years ago. What is wrong with me? Why do I have this insane jealousy toward my son? I just can't have him out of my sight or I go crazy!"

Katherine had sought assistance from conventional counselors, but she had never been satisfied with the results. A friend suggested that she ask us for past-life guidance.

Through our relaxation techniques and guided regression, Katherine moved back through the purple mist of time to view herself in a marital relationship with her son, Philip. They had been man and wife in Milan, Italy, in the 1880s.

Although theirs had been a relatively pleasant marriage, it had been complicated by her intense jealousy of Philip, a medical doctor who was very popular with his female patients. The fear that he might have been having a series of affairs with rich and fashionable women had ceaselessly tormented her, even though her husband had never given her any serious reason to doubt his faithfulness.

When we brought Katherine back to full wakefulness, we spent quite some time with her in consultation. We had to bring her to the realization that she and Philip had been reunited so that a new dimension might be added to their loving relationship. Jealousy could not be part of the present. How truly unfortunate it was that a past-life memory had surfaced to complicate their mother-son experience.

"If only I had known such things sooner," Katherine sobbed. "How can I possibly make amends to my son for what I have done to him?"

These are the great, heartrending questions for which there are no easy answers.

We can only urge everyone to look beyond personal prejudices and be open to explore techniques of extended awareness. Looking within for the answers can prevent cruel errors and actions. If one were to practice the mechanics of extended consciousness from childhood on and learn to seek the guidance to be found in the silence of the inner temple, many thoughtless, tasteless, irresponsible, and hurtful acts could be prevented.

Paul was a compulsive eater. "I am always hungry," he complained. "I can't help it. Every day is one long meal for me."

Paul had once been a handsome, vigorous man. One could still see the vague outline of what had been rugged masculine features. Now they were blurred by the puffiness of his jowls and his sagging chin. He was five feet ten and his body weight had ballooned up to nearly three hundred pounds.

When Paul was deep in regression, we were startled to hear the whimpering sounds of a small child coming from somewhere in the cavern of his chest.

Within moments Paul was describing a life as a poor beggar boy, struggling for subsistence in the crowded streets of Bombay. He told us that he was so hungry, always hungry. He begged us for the smallest scrap of food, the thinnest crust of bread.

Paul died before puberty in that wretched existence. Somehow, something in his present-life experience had triggered those awful memories.

We brought Paul back to his present life, then began progressing him forward from the birth experience.

At age twenty-four we found him in Viet Nam, out on a patrol. Because of the resultant chaos after an attack on the base, Paul was temporarily forgotten. Paul's orders had been to maintain his position at a certain point and not to stray from that area. He had been sent to the position with scant rations, for in the original plan Paul would be replaced within a matter of a few hours.

It was fortunate that Paul had access to some drinkable water, for he was left there unattended for nearly three days. A very hungry Paul was at last brought back to the main camp. He had no sooner begun to eat when they were hit by a barrage of mortar fire that continued for hours.

After the explosions ceased the camp went on full alert to be prepared for what they felt would be an immediate attack.

By the time Paul got a full meal he was nearly famished; and it had been this experience of extreme hunger in his present life that had given rebirth to his past-life memories of a time when hunger was a way of life for him.

After we returned Paul to complete consciousness we

discussed the matter of his compulsive hunger very honestly and earnestly. We recommended that he see a medical doctor at once and begin a sincere program of shedding the many excess pounds. We also promised that we would assist him by providing a conditioning tape that would help him to keep his resolution to lose weight.

From time to time many of us have been beset by compulsions, irrational needs or desires that impinge upon certain situations in our lives. At the least these conditions may have embarrassed us or placed us in awkward circumstances. At the worst these compulsions may have caused us enormous stress and personal conflict.

Very often it is exceedingly difficult to trace the origins of these compulsions. Too often one finds that the memory of why one feels so strongly about a particular person, place, thing, or attitude is completely clouded. While it is perplexing in many cases to explain the origin of a compulsion in your present life, if you are open to an experiment, you may be able to determine the source of the compulsion in a past-life experience.

Lie or sit comfortably and allow yourself to relax as completely as possible. Take a deep breath and hold it for the count of three. Slowly exhale. Repeat this breathing procedure three times.

Contemplate the nature of your compulsion.

Focus as completely as you can on the emotions that seem most affected when this compulsion seizes you. Recall as totally as you can the physical responses that your body undergoes when you experience this compulsion.

Permit yourself to flow back into that experience and try to capture it in your mind's eye as if it were occurring at the present moment.

Answer the following questions as honestly as possible:

What *first* triggered the compulsion within you? Was it the sight of someone or something?

Was it a sound, a word?

Was it an attitude that someone expressed?

Was it a gesture, a movement?

Was it a sensation, a feeling?

Was it due to your touching something?

After the first grips of the compulsion, what did you or anyone else say to cause the irrational activity to continue?

Was there a specific area in your body where you felt a particular physical tension or discomfort? Did the compulsion become so intense that you experienced nausea, dizziness, trembling, a fainting spell?

Were you aware of a specific place in your body where you reacted to the seizure more than any other? Reflect for a moment on that precise spot.

With this assessment in your mind, consider what person in all the world you would least like to be aware of your compulsion. Focus now on that person.

Imagine how this person would react if he or she learned of your compulsion.

See clearly that person's facial expressions. Imagine what physical reactions you would expect from that person. Fantasize what that person would say to you.

As your fantasies sharpen on that person, imagine that individual looking different from his or her present physical appearance. Fantasize that person wearing clothing from some other historical era.

Continuing with the fantasy, project yourself to that same historical period. Scrutinize your own physical appearance. You, too, may be somewhat different in appearance.

Continue to permit your fantasy to evolve. Imagine that you and that person are involved with one another in a very unique and intimate way. Explore the particular relationship you had with that person in that lifetime.

See yourself involved in some especially unique or intimate act with this person. See if this is somehow linked with your compulsion.

Were you punished for this act?

Did you receive censure for this act?

Did you receive approval for this act?

Did you receive praise and encouragement to repeat this act?

What was there that was so attractive to you about this act, this person?

Did the activity turn sour or did it continue to be enjoyable?

Explore as completely as you can the consequences of that act and your involvement with that person. Visualize a scene that left you with a powerful feeling about that act, that attitude, that person. See clearly the connection between this scene and the compulsion you experience in your soul's present expression.

Now fantasize that you are explaining matters to the person you would least like to know of your compulsion.

Visualize that person as he or she appears in this lifetime and in a prior-life experience.

Fantasize an overlap of personalities as you state the facts of your case. Imagine that others have gathered to hear your report.

After you have made as complete an explanation as possible, hear the person and the rest of the gathered audience give their approval.

Hear them as they all say that they understand and accept your explanation.

Hear the person you have associated with your compulsion acknowledge that you have recognized one of the lessons you have returned to learn.

Feel warm waves of unconditional love wash over your body.

Know that on the soul level you have gained a greater perspective on your compulsion. Be aware that on the conscious level you have gained greater knowledge in dealing with your compulsion.

Acknowledge that you need never yield to the compulsion again.

12

Healing Miracles Can Be Yours

Although at no time have we ever declared ourselves to be "healers" in the sense that most people use that term, we have been privileged to serve as the channels for some remarkable healings during the course of several past-life and awareness explorations.

There was the time when three women carried in their older sister, who had suffered from double vision and partial paralysis of her legs for over twelve years. After the woman had experienced a linkup with her Karmic Counterpart, she was not only able to walk straight and unassisted, she was able to dance the tarantella as her joyful sisters clapped and sang her accompaniment.

Once while a subject was deep in a trance, her arm began to move as if it were an independent entity. We frowned at one another in puzzlement as this occurred twice more during her awareness session. She awakened in tears of happiness and went straight to the telephone to call her doctor with the news that the arm that had been paralyzed for three years had now been fully restored.

A man who for several years had been unable to turn his neck because of fused vertebrae, awakened from his regression session laughing and swiveling his head freely from side to side.

There is no need to continue the list interminably. Our purpose is not to impress you with our gifts but to inform you of the ability that lies latent within you that will permit you to heal yourself and to bless others by acting as a channel of healing energy from the God force. In each of the above cases—and in all the many instances we have not recounted—our sole purpose lay in assisting the subject to achieve balance. In fact, in only one or two obvious instances did we even know that the man or woman we had placed in an altered state of consciousness had a physical malady.

We may have caused certain energies to flow more completely and to achieve a better balance within the physical bodies of these subjects. We may have accomplished this through the linkup that occurs when past-life knowledge puts the subject in touch with greater facets of him/herself. We may simply have permitted the subject to relax for the first time in years, thereby allowing certain neural blockages to eliminate themselves. The *how* or the *why* is never as important to us as the end result, especially when we are dealing in matters as undefinable as the farthest reaches of the human psyche.

The Universe is governed by laws that never fail, by forces that work without human consciousness. These energies, these powers, go beyond the present understanding of all humankind, but humankind does have the psychic ability to tap the powers governed by these laws. We have the ability to utilize the infinite currents that surround us and to absorb them into our own bodies.

It is this, the free will by which we can choose to tap into and absorb these energies, that divides us from other animals. But few of us utilize these forces to aid our lives. Few of us know how.

Our superconscious mind, more commonly called the soul, has eternal awareness, eternal consciousness, eternal wisdom, and eternal existence. We have within us the ability to tune into a mind more powerful than our own, whose boundaries are without limits, whose awareness is the Universe. With access to all of this we need not want for anything. Throughout the ages our most revered leaders, master teachers, and prophets have told us of these universal powers that can make us perform miracles.

In the East Indian philosophy of yoga the human body is divided into seven zones. The yogic art of meditation, combined with body control, permits one to achieve with ease those feats which in the Western world would be considered impossible.

There are voluntary and involuntary muscles of the body; through yoga one learns to control both groups. But this physical control is not spirituality, for the serious student of yoga combines humankind's three basic natures into one and then establishes inner control over that one force.

There exist within each of us mental, physical, and spiritual natures. Learning to utilize these as one is the highest form of control over oneself. Everyone is a divine instrument, capable of sending and receiving energy. Our sensory organs would best be described as receivers, for through them we receive sensory input, vibrations of various types. Our mind controls whether we will send or receive energy.

There also exists within us the ability to perceive beyond our five senses; this is known as extrasensory perception. All humans have this sixth sense, as do many lower animals. It has been conjectured that the sixth sense was perhaps far more developed in primitive humankind and that it contributed to the survival of the species. The sixth sense may have provided us with the ability to sense danger, giving us the necessary foreknowledge to escape.

The seven zones of the body are governed by neuro-hormonal energy centers known as chakras. These seven chakra centers emanate from the spine. Opening these seven chakras, permitting them to operate at their fullest capacity, gives you total control over the mental, physical, and spiritual selves. There are various methods whereby you can learn to control your energy, directing it toward the chakra of your choice.

The exercises included in this chapter will show you how to tap into and direct the universal energies, channeling them through your body, achieving whatever you desire.

The seven chakras begin with the base of the spine, the sex glands. The first of the energy centers controls the male and female generative organs of life. Keep in mind the polarity of all energies that exist on the physical plane. The negative applications of the first energy center are anger, greed, and lust.

The second energy center is in the lower abdomen and it controls your body's lower portion, more specifically your legs and hips.

For a moment center your attention on this chakra in the lower abdomen. Close your eyes and feel the energy come into that area and emanate from it. You should be able to feel, even at this early time, a tingling vibration in your legs. The control of your lower body, its functioning and malfunctioning, comes from this chakra.

The third chakra is in the upper abdomen. This center controls the upper abdominal region, affecting all abdominal functions. This center, like the others, restores balance and harmony and cleanses all that it governs.

The fourth chakra is in the midchest. It is the very center of your nervous system. This is known as the heart chakra. This particular center is blocked in many individuals, for their mental and spiritual awareness does not encompass unconditional universal love. With others this chakra center is only partially open, having been opened by the love of one more living thing. To cause this center to operate at its fullest capacity with balance and harmony, you must unconditionally, nonjudgmentally love all living things. An imbalance will cause various ills and malfunctions.

The fifth chakra is in the neck and it controls and balances the upper torso. It affects your communication. When this area is not open or is imbalanced, you can lose control. This chakra influences not only the arms and throat but sensitivity to pressures, currents of energies, temperatures, et cetera. Balancing and opening this energy center permits you further control of many of the glands and organs of your body.

The sixth chakra is what is commonly known as the "third eye," or individual consciousness.

Close your physical eyes and permit the magnetic waves to pulsate into this region between your eyebrows. Fix your attention on this center of energy. Not only will you balance your physical body, you will begin to contact your spiritual self. Continued contact with your spiritual self will put you in contact with another very important part of your being, your soul. This is known as the eye of wisdom. Through this eye you will learn detachment from the physical world and grow in harmony with the cosmos. Through this chakra you will learn to become one with the supreme consciousness that flows throughout the Universe. It is through this third eye that all that exists will be made known to you.

The last chakra is the seventh, the ultimate controller. When you learn to open, govern, and balance this chakra, the individuality that separates you from all of life will disappear. You will become one with the God force, one with the Source of all things, one with God. From this awareness, you will attain eternal life, peace, wisdom, knowledge, and superconsciousness. It is this chakra that permits you *full* and total contact with your higher self, your soul. This state of oneness with the Universe is known in East Indian philosophy as "Nirvana."

Now that you are aware of the energies available to you and know of the centers in your own body through which these forces can be channeled, you are ready to learn mastery of your mind, body, and spirit and to assume total control of your life.

First, be certain that all of your bodily needs have been acknowledged. Wear comfortable, loose clothing. Place your body in a comfortable position, sitting straight-legged on a cushion with your back against the wall, or in lotus posture or lying down. Soft background music will aid you. You may wish to have someone read this to you or make a tape of this method.

With eyes closed begin breathing comfortably, deeply, slowly. Your breathing is getting slower now, slower now. Breathe for several minutes, clearing negative thoughts and all impurities from your body. Become sensitive to the coolness of the air that enters your nostrils and the warmness of the air that leaves. Concentrate on this sensation for at least a minute. Breathe very deeply.

Feel yourself leaving the lower existence for the higher existence.

Feel yourself leaving the darkness for the light.

Feel yourself leaving physical restrictions and rising to eternal immortality. You are leaving the unreal world for the true reality.

Repeat the following suggestions mentally and feel the sensations throughout your body:

"I am relaxing my entire body. Beginning with my feet, legs, torso, arms, neck, face, and head, my entire body is relaxing, becoming more relaxed, more relaxed. My breathing is getting deeper now, deeper now, slower. I am completely relaxed.

"I am aware of the electromagnetic energies that surround me. I can feel these energies all around me. My entire body is bathed in the electromagnetic energies of the Universe. An ocean of superconsciousness awaits me, coming nearer and nearer.

"With every beat of my heart, the energies of the

Universe pulsate within me. I can feel the energies pulsating all around me, throbbing with my own life flow.

"With a deep breath I draw these energies into me, into me. I feel them come into my very being, nurturing me, nourishing every gland and cell of my body, filling me completely. Each breath that I take draws more of the universal energies into me, and I am full of the electromagnetic energies of the Universe.

"My mind is gathering these energies together and focusing them at the very base of my spine. I feel all the energies collecting at the very base of my spine, humming, tingling, vibrating, and opening my first chakra. I feel my first chakra opening, opening, becoming positive and balanced.

"The energies are traveling up my spine and bursting into my second chakra, my abdominal chakra. I can feel my abdomen and my legs become balanced now, in harmony now with all that is positive.

"Now the universal magnetic energies are traveling up into my upper abdomen, my stomach region, and I can feel my third chakra open. I feel balance, harmony, and health fill my being as my third chakra opens and becomes energized.

"Universal magnetic energy is traveling further up my spine to my fourth chakra. It is entering the very center of my nervous system. It is entering my heart, and I can feel my heart open, open wider now, become balanced, more balanced, opening wider. Love, unconditional love, love for all that is, for all living things, for all of life, for God, for the Universe, enters my being. My fourth chakra is open and I feel the energy enveloping me, warming me; and I am filled with love as I've never experienced it—a deeper, more complete love.

"Now, the magnetic energy is going farther up my spine to my fifth energy center, my fifth chakra, in my throat region. I can feel the energy entering, entering now, opening, opening now. The energy is filling my being and I can feel it humming, vibrating, pulsating throughout my entire body. It is balancing me more completely and I will be able to receive and give energies more fully. It is balancing many of my glandular functions. My fifth energy center is open.

"The magnetic universal energies are rushing into the area between my brows, my third-eye region, my sixth chakra. I can feel the magnetic waves pulsating, tingling, throbbing. The energy feels wonderful. It feels so beautiful.

"A light before me is getting larger and larger now. The light is growing larger still and opening larger still, until it covers the entire vision of my third eye.

"I am aware of my spirit, and I feel my spirit within me moving. It is freer, becoming detached from the physical. It is leaving the physical, lesser, reality for the truer, spiritual, all encompassing reality. I feel one—one with all that is, one with the Universe. I can now reach the higher consciousness that governs the entire Universe. I desire to know all, for I seek the Source of all that is.

"The energy is now blossoming forth in my brain, like a thousand-petaled lotus blossom, opening up, petal by petal, one after the other.

"I feel the energies filling my mind completely, totally, fully. I am in balance completely. My entire being is in balance, in harmony with all that is and with the Universe. I am reaching for my higher self, my higher consciousness, my personal superconsciousness, my soul. I can feel its energies entering my being. I merge into it. My soul merges into me. We are one. We are one.

"From this day forth I vow forever to reflect my higher self, my soul, in all that I do. As I am merged into it and it is one with me, all things known by it are available to me. I am one with my higher self in the timeless realm. All love, wisdom, and knowledge can now be gathered here and I desire to know many things. I thirst, and I shall be quenched. I hunger, and I shall be fulfilled!

Past Life and Rainbow Cloud Healing Technique

Use one of the methods of relaxation described elsewhere in this book or any successful technique of your own to place yourself in a deep level of consciousness. Have someone read the following suggestions to you or, as advised previously, prerecord the suggestions and serve as your own guide via cassette tape.

You are so peaceful, so beautifully relaxed. You glance up into the blue, blue sky and pick the most attractive cloud that you can see. It is a rather small cloud, but it is exquisitely formed. It is a beautiful cloud with magnificent peaks.

You feel deeply at peace, looking upward at the cloud's fluffiness, its thick, rich fullness. It is soft and white, and it appears to be glowing . . . as it catches the rays of sunlight and shines with beautiful, prismatic colors.

As you watch the cloud, you wish to ride upon it, knowing that this special cloud would hold you safely in space. If you mounted the cloud, you would be able to soar above the trees, the town, the cities, Earth itself. You would be able to move into the heavens themselves. You could enjoy the beauty of the twinkling stars.

You could move close to the stars. You might be able to reach out and touch them. As you moved higher, the air would be fresh and pure. It would be a new world, a higher dimension. All would be so wonderful.

The cloud appears to be growing larger and larger . . . larger still. And you notice that it appears to be floating toward you. You are happy inside. Perhaps someone up there heard your wish, for the cloud is lowering itself to you. You know that you will soon be able to climb aboard.

The cloud settles down right next to you. You know that you may now climb safely aboard. You easily step over a puffy rim into the soft, fluffy center of the cloud. It is so comfortable on the cloud, so peaceful. And you can lie back as if you are lying down in an incredibly comfortable reclining chair.

Your cloud is so soft, so strong, so secure.

A ray of light shines forth from the heavens and touches your strong and fluffy cloud. It causes your cloud to glow softly. The radiance is different from any other light that you have ever seen. You can feel it as well as see it. It feels strangely wonderful, and it causes you to become very happy within yourself.

You know that you have felt this sensation before. Sometime before in your life it has touched your heart. It is the warmth of love . . . a beautiful, touching love. You feel so at peace, so happy, so loved. You begin to rise . . . floating slowly, gently, so very safely.

You know that you are protected by love from a higher power.

You begin to drift . . . drift and float . . . gently bobbing along like a cork in a pond. Drifting and floating. Drifting and floating. Higher and higher still.

As you drift . . . drift and float, you glance easily down toward the Earth. You can see the trees . . . the countryside . . . the cities and towns growing smaller and smaller until they look like tiny toys on a green blanket.

You are rising higher and higher, far above the ground. Smell the fresh winds as the air becomes fresher, cleaner, the higher you go. You breathe deeper and deeper, deeper and deeper, and you settle back comfortably on your cloud to rest and to enjoy the feelings of peace and love all around you.

You are floating higher, higher, and higher. You are floating out of this time, out of this place, far out into the dimension from whence came that ray of beautiful light that made your cloud glow. You are going to that place in space where the warm, glowing light emanates.

There is an opening ahead and it is coming closer and closer. You slip through the opening.

You can see now that it is not merely an opening, but a tunnel, a tunnel filled with myriad designs. And there is a light at the far, far end. See the light far ahead at the end of the tunnel.

The designs are sliding past you on all sides. Three-dimensional octagons are moving above you, beneath you, and on either side of you. Notice how perfectly these eight-sided objects are made.

Now you are speeding to the light at the end of the tunnel, barely noticing the designs. You are moving to that place in space where there is no time at all. You are coming swiftly to the end of the tunnel and you slip easily through it into a strange and glorious place. This is a place that exists beyond time.

Now see before you a panaroma of Earth from its beginning to the present date. Concentrate on the area of your body that is painful, diseased, or malfunctioning. See in your mind that particular body part about which you desire to know more.

Be aware that in that great expanse of time that lies before you your soul has led a particular lifetime that is directly affecting your body in the present. Whether it was a life experience that existed thousands of years ago, hundreds of years ago, a few generations back, or even if it was a forgotten event in your present lifetime, you have the ability to see before you the lifetime and the event that caused your present problem.

You have the ability to see that lifetime and to know all that occurred during that experience.

You will see all that transpired to cause the problem that so troubles you. See it. Know it. Understand it. Remember it. (Permit yourself approximately two minutes to contemplate your images and memories.)

Now you understand why you are suffering this problem. You see and know why the problem has come about. You are happy to have discovered where its roots lie.

And now, with the vibrations of this awareness, and with firm resolve to right all wrongs, to better existing circumstances, you are strengthened and know that you can be healed. You are wiser and stronger now, and you know deep within your heart that you can be released from the grasp of this event. You can be healed.

You glance down toward the east where a light, misty rain is falling, and you watch the sunlight sparkle through the tiny raindrops, which are transformed as if by magic into a myriad of sparkling diamonds. A beautiful rainbow appears, a rainbow that you know can heal you. The rainbow is formed from the colorful, prismatic glitter. See the stretching bands of lilac, rich lilac; rose, soft, beautiful rose; green, vibrant green; and sparkling, glowing gold before you. So beautiful. So near you.

You desire to pass through the healing rainbow upon your cloud and to feel the colors move all around and through you. You are going closer now, closer and closer. The rain has ceased, but the rainbow remains crisp and clear. You will start with the bottom color of gold and work up through all the colors to lilac.

You are passing into the gold—a glowing, sunny gold that touches your very being. You breathe much more deeply now, more freely now, as gold enters your body. You can see it all around you, warm and glowing. Gold is all around you and through you. Gold is going through you and you feel love enter your heart, mind, and body. You are now leaving gold and you enter into green.

Green—a very rich, living, healing green. Green as a fresh leaf. Feel and see the green all around you. Green passing through you, healing you, inside and out. Green, healing your scars, wounds, pains, and troubles. A warmer loving sensation fills your being, and you leave green and pass into rose.

Rose, a delicate shade of rose, a pinkish shade of rose, so lovely, so beautiful. Rose all around you. Rose passing through you. You feel your heart being bathed in rose. Your heart is softer now, more pliable now, expanding and filling with an even richer, more beautiful love. You are leaving rose now and passing into velvety lilac.

Lilac—the most beautiful shade of lilac you've ever seen. Lilac all around you. Lilac passing through you. You feel yourself glow lilac, as your body is growing stronger and stronger, your love is growing deeper and deeper.

You are passing out of the lilac and leaving the rainbow. Before you, beaming down from the heavens is a rich, elegant shade of violet. Bright, glowing violet that is pulsating with life. Yes, the universal lifeforce is reaching down to you from the sky. It is touching your body.

You see violet, bright, glowing, pulsating all around you, and you feel it within you. Violet is pulsating through your entire being. You can feel the lifeforce within you, and it feels so wonderful, so powerful, so beautiful, so good. You feel yourself being filled with the most beautiful, perfect love that could possibly exist. Love, true love as it was always meant to be. Unconditional love. Nonjudgmental love. Love without any conditions placed upon it. And this unconditional love fills your being. Love such as this exists throughout the universe. This love will sustain you in any crisis.

Now you see before you the Earth as a round ball. See the Earth beneath you suspended in space as a round blue ball. You are far above it, filled with love, unconditional love, perfect love.

Now imagine yourself as a kettle, complete with a spout, just as a tea kettle would be. The spout is where your heart is. Let your love pour out of your heart. Pour it forth from the spout, where your heart is, and see it pouring over all the Earth, over everything living. Pour it over all lifeforms that exist, over all people, all animals, all life.

Pour forth your love over all living things and feel the violet ray of love energy touch you again and fill you once again with unconditional love. Feel it flow into you as you pour it out of you, pouring through you. As you pour, so you receive from above, giving and receiving unconditional love.

You will always permit this love to flow into you and pour from you, to pour through you. You will be an instrument of this love vibration through the giving of this love. You feel strong, stronger than you've ever felt before. You feel healed within as well as without. You are clean, refreshed, balanced. You are renewed mentally, spiritually, and physically.

You will practice giving unconditional love from this day forth. You will give unconditional love to all living things when you awaken and before you go to sleep at night. You will give unconditional love throughout all your life and receive it afresh, anew. You feel whole, balanced, healed within and without.

You are beginning to descend. Your cloud is beginning to descend, going down, down, down, down to Earth. You are returning to Earth. Down, down, down. Back to Earth. You will remember all that you've seen, realized, and experienced.

On the count of six all of your six senses will awaken, and be made more perfect. *One,* your sense of taste . . . *Two,* your sense of smell . . . *Three,* your hearing . . . *Four,* your touch . . . *Five,* your sight . . . and *Six,* the most important of all, your intuition, your extrasensory perception, now awakens. Awake, refreshed, positive, healed, balanced, and filled with love, unconditional love for all.

13

Achieving True Sexual Satisfaction

Julia and Dick were very frank with us. They had nothing good between them but sex.

"To be brutally honest," Julia sighed, nervously clicking her long, brightly-colored nails against the arm of the chair, "our married life has been nothing but a cycle of depression, boredom, and violent fights. Hell, we've nearly killed each other a couple of times."

"Julia doesn't mean we're murderers or anything," Dick felt compelled to explain. "She busted a lamp over my head once, and I've smacked her good a couple of times. Nothing really deadly serious."

But serious enough that they wanted to stop it.

"That's right," Julia agreed. "And either shape up our marriage or end it."

Had they considered divorce?

"More times than I can count," Dick told us.

What seemed most often to set off the fights and quarrels?

"Just the good old national problem: money!" Julia supplied.

"Well, honey," Dick corrected her. "The national averages say *two* things most often set off marital disputes: sex and money. We never fight about sex. We just do it!"

"Like I said, folks," Julia smiled somewhat sheepishly, "sex is what has held our marriage together. And we sincerely would like to see if we can't get more out of our marriage."

Did they both agree on that reason for having made an appointment with us?

"Sure," Dick told us. "When that is so good, it is a shame that the rest of our marriage has to be so bad. If we can make it better, I am definitely for it."

We took our time relaxing Julia and Dick, since it was obvious that they were both somewhat distraught. With our voices working together creating a relaxed atmosphere, we first took the couple to a higher level of consciousness where they might encounter their guides. This proved to be a very profound experience for both of them. Tears streamed down their cheeks and there was a soft, sad-happy sound of audible sobbing.

Once this psychic reunion had occurred, we suggested that they ask their guides to permit them to view past-life scenes that would provide them with definite clues to their present-life problem of marital incompatibility.

Within moments we had moved with Julia and Dick back through the purple mist of time, and we were with them in New Orleans at the turn of the century.

The expression of Julia's soul at that time in history described herself as a young girl who had been sent to the city to obtain better schooling than her rural area could provide. She had no sooner established herself in the boarding school than she made the acquaintance of a tall, handsome man who was the entity we now knew as Dick.

Although her friends warned her that he was a wanderer, Julia found him fascinating, so very different from the clumsy lads she had left behind in the small town she came from. Their relationship progressed on a far more rapid course than she could have predicted, and she was more astonished than ashamed when she surrendered her virginity to his seductive prowess.

But she became like a kitten suddenly turned on to catnip. Her studies began to matter little to her. She craved the sexual attention from the exciting man in her life. Dick seemed to have no end of inventive love techniques, and he also provided her with alcohol, a vice that had been strictly denied the young girl.

Then, on an awful night of delirium when she was dizzy with drink, Dick left her alone with another man.

Julia was heartsick when she fully recovered her senses. She loved only Dick. She could not understand what had happened. She had not meant to let the other man take advantage of her. She begged for Dick's forgiveness and understanding.

Dick laughed at her sniveling, for he had arranged the rendezvous—for cash.

Before the shocked, humiliated Julia could protest, Dick had brought her to an apartment where two girls about her own age were living. He introduced them as his other girls. He would be their protector. They would make love to men whom he selected, and they would do it on a nightly basis.

When Julia protested, Dick beat her unconscious, though he was careful to strike her only where the bruises could easily be hidden.

And so their relationship had continued for years. Although Julia had come to despise Dick and had once even tried to kill him with a straight-edged razor, she seemed to require his brutal love-making. Until her death at the hands of a drunken stevedore, Julia lived as Dick's sexual slave.

After we brought Julia and Dick back to full consciousness, we left them alone for a few minutes, permitting them to reemerge in this lifetime while listening to soft music on our cassette player. When we re-entered our office with some iced tea, Dick could barely meet our eyes when he spoke.

"Hey, you know, I'm really not that kind of guy. I've never been into anything kinky, and I've never *really* walloped Julia—or any other woman for that matter! And there's no way that I would ever want to share her body with other men!"

"Jeez," Julia shook her head. "What about that? Do you think that really happened to us?"

We asked them how they felt about that. Did it feel like an experience that could fit their life together?

"It was so remarkable," Dick had to admit. "I mean, it *was* Julia—and it wasn't. You know, it . . . she . . . didn't look much like Julia today, yet somehow I knew it was Julia."

"And all those details." Julia was still shaking her head in disbelief. "I really *saw* that girls' boarding school. I saw my classmates there. And I agree with Dick: I knew that the man I was falling in love with *was* Dick, even though it didn't really look like him. Dick is taller—"

"But I was thinner then," Dick added.

"And I can't imagine you would ever part your hair in the middle," Julia giggled.

"Or wear one of those pointed moustaches." Dick joined her amusement. "Or wear those awful striped shirts!"

"Hey," Julia suddenly realized. "Isn't it incredible, Dick? We both saw you the same way. How about me?"

"Your hair was blond then instead of brunette," Dick told her. "But you dyed it red after I . . . after I set you up in business."

"That's what I saw, too!" Julia agreed. "And I was a bit too plump then."

Dick shrugged. "Pleasingly plump, I think they called it in those days. Hey, that is really something how we could go into two separate altered states yet both see the same images. We must have seen an actual past-life memory of ours."

We pointed out that in our understanding it was not that important whether the experience they had shared had been a true past life. If it seemed real and true to them, that was what was important.

But, the bottom line was whether or not the vision they had shared would help them achieve a more total and compatible marital adjustment.

"I really think so," Dick answered. "I mean, I now have a totally different perspective."

We told him that was what we had hoped to provide: a new perspective from which to view their problem.

"Yeah," Julia agreed with her husband. "After all, honey, we really have so many things on which we can build our marriage—other than bedsprings."

In our discussion with Julia and Dick, we were careful to establish the awareness that their spiritual evolution had progressed beyond that earlier lifetime. They had come together again so that they might enter a love vibration of deeper value. It had only been a past-life memory that had held them to that more primitive method of expressing love. This time their challenge was to rise above the genital level of pure animal instinct, and to guide one another into a more complete and supportive love.

Sexual Satisfaction from Channeled Energy

As science has proven, energy exists in *all* matter, in *every* living thing. The human mind is a most amazing instrument, for it can tap, channel, and utilize energy, thereby affecting the physical body.

We live in a three-dimensional reality, and when we tap into and channel this energy and allow it into our own energy systems (our chakras), we cause it to affect our three-dimensional selves—our mental, physical, and spiritual selves—our personal Universe.

In our three-dimensional reality energy can be *positively*

channeled and utilized—or *negatively* channeled and utilized. How it is used in our world is really up to us. This free will permits us to be the governors of this energy in our own Universe, our own reality. We truly dictate the way we will use this energy. We alone are responsible for causing it to be positive or negative. We are the dictators of it; we are the gods of it; we are the controllers of it.

Positively used energy raises our vibrations on three levels within our systems—the mental, the physical, and the spiritual—ultimately permitting us to blend with the highest energy, the Source. Negatively used energy lowers our vibrations on all three levels, shutting us off from the highest vibration of the Source of all things.

The negative utilization of energy through any one of our energy centers, any one of our chakras, adversely affects the particular region or zone that particular chakra governs, eventually affecting the entire system by lowering its vibratory level.

For instance, if the energy of love that exists in your heart is restricted to love for individuals who meet certain conditions, this restriction causes the heart to fail to vibrate to its fullest capacity. This restriction causes it to begin to malfunction, eventually affecting the entire circulatory system, the complete electrical system of the body. On the other hand, the ability to express nonjudgmental love and to utilize this energy within your heart, giving it to all living things unconditionally, permits the energy to operate at its fullest, most powerful, and most balanced. Unconditional love allows the heart to vibrate with full health, to become a rhythmically tuned organ, thus resulting in a perfect circulatory system and consequently, total health.

Through a simple mental exercise you can master control of the universal energy and channel it through your own personal energy system. You have the ability to open, to magnify, and to energize your seven chakras, thereby balancing your Universe, your temple within, mentally, physically, and spiritually.

On the physical plane you can easily feel the immediate effect of the universal energy when it is being directed into your own first energy system, your sexual chakra.

Close your eyes and quiet your entire body for one or two minutes. Mentally imagine the gathering of the energy that exists in all of matter. See it moving toward your crown chakra. Imagine it coming to you and entering your head. Feel it traveling down your spine and bursting into your first chakra, your sexual region.

Again, *imagine* it, *gather* it, *channel* it down your spine. Feel it burst into your sexual chakra.

Again, *imagine, channel, feel,* and *let it burst* into your first chakra.

Do this over and over, permitting waves of energy to enter you, to flow down you and through you and to burst into your first chakra. This will produce pleasurable feelings.

This is the easiest area in which to feel the immediate effect of energy, for it is a most sensitive zone. It is an energy center that demands, even commands, our attention throughout our lives, for it is a very important area for the existence of animal life on our planet. It controls the male and female reproductive systems so that we replicate ourselves. By channeling the energy into your first chakra, your sexual zone, you will learn how to master the channeling of energy into and through your remaining chakras, thereby raising them into finer attunement.

In this, the world of polarities, where energy manifests positively or negatively due to our own direction, the first chakra is the easiest of the seven to energize. The need for new life favors this energy, but since it is the easiest to energize, it is the hardest to control. But control it you must, for the energy that can be created by this center, if channeled negatively, can result in great destruction, sexual perversion, frustrating lust, and greed, with ensuing anger and chaos.

The heart chakra is an energy system that, when mastered with love, will permit you positive control over your sexual chakra, for it aids all the chakras. Utilizing the heart chakra and the sexual chakra together causes the energy to be governed positively, magnifying it to its fullest capacity, intensifying it to its greatest height.

That is why we enjoy sex far more with someone we *love*, why it is more beautiful and complete. And that is also why sex becomes mechanical with those we do not love, for the act then becomes only a form of masturbation, to release the existing energy in this center through robotlike manipulation.

Experiencing the unconditional love energy in the heart chakra is a beautiful feeling in itself. Blending it with the sexual energy magnifies your sexual enjoyment. This, too, is a rather easy exercise to enjoy when first performed. With continued practice the ultimate pleasure will result, for it becomes more perfected, more controlled.

Close your eyes, quiet your entire body, relaxing it from head to toe for a few minutes.

Now imagine above you the energy within all that exists. Imagine that you are gathering this energy from the four corners of the Universe. See it gathering from the north, coming to the center of the heavens directly above you. (Imagining the energy aids you in tapping it, utilizing it, eventually controlling it.) Now imagine it coming from the south, from the east, and from the west, gathering together, blending into one glowing ball of bright, golden energy.

Imagine this energy coming down toward you, coming down and pouring into your head, entering your crown chakra. Think positively; think of the most positive of all things, the highest thought available to you. Think of unconditional love for all living things, nonjudgmental love, and feel this energy travel down your spine positively, like a thick, warming, glowing, tingling energy, filling you, making you feel complete, whole.

Imagine it pouring into the heart area, filling your heart completely.

Imagine before you the one you love. Now permit the

energy to continue to travel down your spine and enter into your sexual region, your first chakra. Permit it to fill this region.

Feel it glow. Permit the two energy systems to vibrate together—your heart chakra imagining your loved one before you, and your sexual chakra. Feel it harmonize, blend, and glow as one.

Again gather the energy, and notice how it continues to collect and to pour in waves into your crown chakra. See and feel the waves of energy enter you. Think of unconditional love for all living things. Feel it in your heart. Think of your love. Feel it enter your sexual region.

Continue this process over and over. Feel how your sexual energy has been modified, magnified, glorified.

Throughout the day and into the early evening hours—or whenever you wish to prepare for sexual enjoyment—perform this mental exercise of blending the heart chakra with the sexual chakra while imagining your mate before you. This should be repeated five or six times at least. You will notice how it takes less time for you to imagine, manifest, and feel the energy travel through your body. You also will notice how it takes less time to perform the entire exercise and how you are becoming more proficient at it.

Moments before sexual intercourse, perform this mental exercise to the fullest strength, permitting it to glow full within you, vibrating your heart and sexual areas to their strongest, most complete capacity. Continue the process throughout the entire sexual act. Feel the waves of energy entering your heart and your sexual areas, while expressing unconditional, all-encompassing love for your mate. Feel the waves of energy gathering and welling up in your heart and your sexual area and becoming one mighty force. Continue this process until you desire to release all of the energy collected within you. Then do so with love.

Obviously, if both partners practice this imagery together, the energy they both generate and exchange with each other becomes so intense that the most beautiful of all sexual feelings will manifest themselves, love and sexuality, the blending of the divine with the material. When the two are balanced, total, positive, complete, and harmonious, they are wondrous to behold.

We could certainly understand Bart's frustration when he brought his attractive wife, Kim, to us for consultation. Tearfully Kim admitted that even though she loved her husband and found him both sexy and considerate, she simply could not enjoy having intercourse with him.

"I just didn't get married to have a brother-sister relationship with Kim," Bart explained. He was a tall, good-looking, muscular man with a good job in a factory. "I wince every time I hear someone tell a joke about 'tonight's the night!' That kind of 'tonight' is so seldom for me that I nearly need a sexual manual to help me remember how!"

Kim was in her early twenties, obviously embarrassed by their reason for coming to us. "I do want a family someday," she admitted, "but..."

"But it might have to be by adoption only." Bart dropped his arms to his sides in frustration. "On those rare occasions when we do have sex, Kim is so uptight that the whole experience is ruined for me. And even though she might not complain verbally after we bumble through it, I can tell by her attitude that she would rather have broken her foot."

Kim and Bart had been to two psychoanalysts, three family counselors, and one psychologist without any successful alleviation of their problem. It was obvious to us that we were once again in the "last resort" category.

We looked at each other and smiled. We told them that we were used to this, and that we understood their reluctance to attempt a solution that most people might consider a bit unorthodox.

When we worked with couples, we often placed both of them in an altered state of deep relaxation and guided them together through a past-life experience that was somehow interfering with their marriage. Generally we would tape such experiences so that the couple could later play the cassette to reinforce the positive programming that always resulted from such a session.

Together, we used our techniques of relaxation to bring both Kim and Bart to a deeper level of consciousness, then we permitted them to encounter their guides. We urged them to ask their guides to permit them to see themselves in a past-life experience they may have shared and which could provide them with clues that might help them understand Kim's present-life problem of frigidity.

Within a few moments Kim and Bart were reexperiencing a life that the two had led in a somewhat primitive time in the Middle East.

They were nomadic people, setting up their tents as they followed their herds of goats. Bart was a wealthy man, the possessor of many horses, hundreds of goats, and six wives. Kim had been one of those wives and all had been circumcised. Bart and Kim relived certain of the unpleasant experiences of that lifetime, but we were careful to keep them as detached and unemotional as possible. We were attempting to solve one crisis situation, not create new ones.

We learned that Bart treated all of his wives as if they were only "baby factories." He was only interested in adding to his prestige and wealth by fathering sons to tend his flocks.

He had impregnated Kim nine times in that prior-life experience, and he had murdered two girl babies before her anguished eyes. Another girl he had sold to a fat merchant when the child was only eleven.

It became increasingly obvious that the karmic carry-over had left Kim reluctant to engage in sexual intercourse with Bart for fear of replicating her "brood mare" status with him. We knew that we had to make it clear to her that she and Bart had been given the opportunity to love again in more enlightened times.

There was just a moment or two of awkward silence after we brought them back to complete wakefulness from their altered states.

"Kim," Bart said softly, taking his wife's hand in his own. "That was horrible. I was the ultimate male chauvinist pig!"

"W-was that really true?" Kim asked us. "I mean did we really live that life? It was awful!"

We explained that we were not interested in proving whether or not the experience they had just relived was their actual past life, or the past life of anyone else for that matter. The importance lay in assessing the vision to see if it bore any clues to their present-life situation.

"It is true," Kim admitted. "Bart has never been anything other than respectful toward me in his lovemaking and in our life together. There has truly been a block there and I know that it is within me. It has nothing to do with Bart."

"Well, it's been pretty hard not to take it personally." Bart grimaced. "I mean, there are just the two of us alone in the bedroom."

Kim told us that she had been a virgin until marriage and that Bart had not pressured her when she explained that she would not yield sexually until they had exchanged vows.

"I took a lot of cold showers," Bart laughed, "but I respected Kim for her moral stand. I had our marriage to look forward to—or so I thought!"

Kim obviously disliked discussing such intimate matters, but she continued her inner unfolding to us. "In spite of the birth control measures available, I have always had a great fear of pregnancy. I mean, it is almost phobic with me. Maybe it is phobic!"

Bart pursed his lips thoughtfully before he spoke. The past life we just saw—or whatever it was that we experienced—that could explain your fear of getting pregnant!"

"Somehow, as much as Bart would say that he loved me and found me the beautiful girl in his dreams, I always felt that deep down inside he only wanted children from me," Kim said softly, a tear moving down her right cheek.

"I've never made any secret of the fact that I wanted kids," Bart said frankly.

"But you frightened me when you said you wanted enough sons to have your own football team!" Kim protested.

We joined Bart's laughter, then commiserated with Kim as he explained to her, "Honey, you must have known I was joking. I mean, wow! Eleven sons! At least three daughters to be cheerleaders!"

Somehow, though, we told the young couple, Bart's continued joking reference to having a large number of children could have stirred deep memories of the primitive lifetime in which she served Bart as a mare for child after child.

"But that was another lifetime," Bart echoed our comments. "Another place. Another you and me!"

Kim nodded. "I can see that now, Bart. I really can. This session with the Steigers has been really valuable. Who could have guessed that I had all that locked inside of me?"

Bart lifted his right hand as if he were taking an oath. "I promise that I'll keep that sex-mad sheik locked up in my soul memory banks forever!"

Joining Former Lifetimes of Love

Throughout the twenty years we've researched past lives, both individually and together, we have discovered that for those couples who feel a deep love for one another—sometimes at their first meeting—there exist many past lives of loving one another that have been shared by their two souls.

Throughout many incarnations their two souls have

joined together in a common goal to aid one another while experiencing life on the Earth plane. Therefore, in several lifetimes they were joined in a common bond of love, frequently in the close relationship of marriage. In most of such cases we also found that these entities were soul mates and that their mission to Earth was a singular one, to be shared by the lives they led.

Therefore, we derived a beautiful method of increasing these individuals' marital relationships on every level—mentally, spiritually, and physically. The technique joins together all the former lifetimes shared by their souls. All positive information gathered by their souls in lifetimes shared on Earth is permitted to gather in the present couple who are performing the exercise. This results in their attaining a higher level of awareness and experiencing the deepest of all emotional loves—together with the physical expression enjoyed throughout many lifetimes. All who have practiced the method have been thrilled with the results. Their lives have been greatly enriched and their enjoyment of the physical act of love has been glorious, surpassing all previous experiences either had ever shared.

This exercise takes some practice; but the results are worth the effort. Your enjoyment begins with your first shared experience, and it gathers momentum until it eventually results in the greatest of all pleasures on every level, physically, mentally, and spiritually.

In a dark room while lying side by side with your partner, stare at the ceiling while quieting your entire body, using whichever muscle-relaxing technique you prefer. Background music with soft percussion instruments (Island or African drums, for instance) suggesting the heartbeats of many lifetimes, is useful. Soft lights or flickering candles should be the only illumination. Relax in this manner for at least six to eight minutes.

Next, close your eyes and fill your body with unconditional love, love for all living things, so that you raise your vibrational energies to the level where you can tap into the memories contained within your soul.

Think of your soul, concentrate on it, feel it, know it; permit it to enter and to glow throughout your body.

See, feel, and know all the many lifetimes your souls have lived together, the loves they have shared.

See, feel, remember all the loves that have existed, all the beautiful feelings shared, and permit this to flow into your consciousness, into your entire being. Feel it filling you and energizing you, awakening every cell in your body. Let flow into you all the love, wisdom, and knowledge shared.

Feel the love, wisdom, and knowledge gathered through-out time filtering into you. The vibrations are the highest. Feel your own energies rise higher and higher.

Feel and share love. Over and over let love play upon your body, play upon your mind. Feel it, thrill to it, share it.

When both of you have been filled with this love, and after about ten to fifteen minutes have passed, turn to blend all the energies with each other, as if in defiance of time and space.

Each time this exercise is performed, more images, memories, and feelings will enter your being; and the period of meditating will become shorter. Eventually all you will need to do is to quiet yourself and relax into a flashback taking just a few minutes, three to five at the most, in order to experience the heights and depths of love, wisdom, knowledge and togetherness.

Even while Bob and Melody were conferring with us, they were playfully teasing each other and attempting to top one another. With their lively competitive minds it was difficult to quiet them long enough to place them in a deep altered state for a mutual regression.

"Whatever the lifetime we experience," Bob commented in mock seriousness, "I know that I will be the superior one. If Melody was a slave, I know I was the master. If she was a famous painter, then I must have been her teacher."

"That would only be fair, Bob," Melody replied, "since you are so obviously inferior to me in this lifetime."

Bob laughed nearly as hard as Melody's joke as she did.

"What do you two think of Melody's new dress?" Bob asked us.

Before we could answer, though, he was moving along with his zinger: "We were nearly late for our appointment because I couldn't pull her out of the Salvation Army Goodwill store. That's where she does all her shopping."

"That's because you are too cheap to give me any money to shop anywhere else," Melody shot back at her husband.

"With a figure like yours, I feel you need the Salvation Army. Your body is lost, but maybe they can still save your soul!"

You should talk, Bob," Melody laughed. "You're getting so fat you'll soon be able to walk down both sides of the street at the same time!"

It was incredible listening to the two of them. We wondered if we should get a pail of cold water to throw on them both.

And it was truly amazing to hear them both laughing good-naturedly at the most pointed of putdowns. They seemed to revel in one another's wit. We knew, though, that eventually one of them would go a bit too far, dig a bit too deeply, feelings would be injured, and a real argument would explode in place of the mock verbal warfare.

That was, in fact, the reason they had made an appointment with us. Their playful jabbing and sparring had resulted in so many serious and prolonged arguments that their marriage was now in jeopardy.

As was our custom when working with couples, we placed the tape recorder between the reclining chairs on which Bob and Melody relaxed. After guiding them into a deep state of altered consciousness, we would tape the experience so that they might later play back the cassette to reinforce the positive programming that resulted.

We at last managed to quiet these two comedians and using the previously mentioned relaxation techniques, we brought them to their guides for a wonderfully moving encounter. Once this union was accomplished, they requested that they be allowed to view themselves in a shared—or single—past-life experience that would help them to understand their unique present-life relationship.

The session soon evolved into a truly remarkable one. The competitive man and wife in the present lifetime had been jealous brothers in old Spanish California in a previous-life experience.

We heard the two quarreling about everything from horses to women. It was clear that the two brothers were rivals in every possible situation—from seeking their parents' affection to their passion for the same woman. They continually fought, both physically and verbally.

But it was also very clear that the two brothers loved each other very much. As if we were listening to a historical novel being played out for us, we heard one of the brothers challenging a wealthy landowner to a duel.

The brother won, but his slaying of the landowner set in motion a bloody vendetta between the two families. The two rival brothers had died defending each other in a climatic battle with the landowner's avenging relatives.

Melody was the first to speak after we had brought them back to full consciousness. "I was a *man* in that life. And I was your brother! Can you believe that, Bob?"

Bob sat in uncharacteristic silence. "Yes, Melody, I can. Isn't that how I've treated you too often? Like one of the boys? Like a brother? Whether we're up at dawn to go fishing or whether we're last off the tennis courts at night, too much of our relationship is like two buddies kidding around with each other."

"At least it hasn't extended to the bedroom," Melody laughed. "You haven't treated me like one of the guys there!"

"I think you're being too kind now," Bob told her. "When I think of our love life, I have to admit that I could be more tender with you, more attentive to you."

Melody lowered her head. "I won't argue with you about that. And I wouldn't turn down that tender, loving care you're talking about either!"

"And it is possible for ours to be an equal marriage in all respects," Bob suggested, "without both of us literally trying to wear the pants and perform the male role."

"You mean I have to stop being a tomboy?" Melody pouted. "I've been a tomboy since I was four years old!"

"Naw, I love you that way," Bob grinned. "I'm just talking about our attitudes toward one another."

Melody agreed. "The important thing is, it appears that I've always loved you...in one form or another!"

Love itself is a beautiful, growing, evolving dimension of awareness. We have each of us loved one another before as husbands and wives, parents and children, brothers and sisters. Love should never stagnate. Love by its very nature must always flow onward.

Resolving Past Life Conflict

Achieve a deep state of relaxation by means of one of the techniques described in this book or a favorite one of your own. Use the prerecorded cassette tape method of serving as your own guide, or have a trusted friend or family member read the following. Or, utilize your own ability to free-associate using the following suggestions while in a relaxed frame of mind.

Ask your guide to take you back through the purple mist of time to a time and a place in which you shared a life experience with the lover or spouse with whom you are having conflict in your present lifetime.

See yourself walking along a street in a city that you recognize, a trail in an area that is familiar, or riding on some road that strikes a responsive memory chord. You recognize the time in which you now exist. You know the place in which you now exist.

You see before you now the home of your beloved. You have just had a quarrel and you feel terrible. Take a moment to analyze your feelings toward your loved one. Take stock of just exactly what your emotions are at this time.

Look at the home of your beloved. Do you share this home with the loved one? Does the loved one live here alone or with someone else?

What plants grow near the walls of the dwelling place? What is there about the immediate area that captures your attention?

What are your expectations as you walk up the path to the dwelling place of your loved one?

Make your presence known at the door or the entrance of the dwelling place. Knock, ring a bell, do whatever is required.

The door is opening. It is your loved one. It is a bright, sunny day and your loved one's features are very clear.

Look closely at your beloved. Become totally aware of this person with whom you are so emotionally linked. See the eyes, the lips, the cheekbones, the forehead, the ears, the hair, the clothes, the body, the way your loved one moves. Has this loved one come with you in your present life?

What expression is there on the loved one's face? Is the loved one happy to see you? Or angry at the very sight of you?

You have brought a present in an effort to end the quarrel. Offer your present to your beloved. Say that you no longer wish to fight.

See what it is that you have brought your loved one. See your loved one's reaction to the gift.

Your beloved indicates that you should step inside the dwelling place. Look around you. See objects in the dwelling place that are familiar to you.

Your loved one gestures that you should be seated. Your loved one stands before you. You hear this dear one say that you will now learn that person's response to your love. You will now hear exactly what your loved one thinks of you and precisely what your future will be with this person. You will know and understand clearly what happened in that past-life relationship that has so affected your present-life interaction with the current soul expression of that entity.

Observe your loved one very closely. Your beloved may communicate with merely a facial expression, a gesture of the hands, or a movement of the body. This knowledge may be presented to you at some length with carefully selected words. You may even be shown an object or a symbol.

However your loved one transmits the knowledge, it will be for your good and your gaining. The loved one is transmitting the information...now. (Pause for about two minutes to receive the images and impressions.)

How do you feel about the decision that your loved one has transmitted? Do you understand how this quarrel and this subsequent pronouncement from your loved one has affected your present-life interaction?

Before you leave, tell your loved one your true feelings about your relationship. How does your beloved react?

As you are walking out the door, your loved one hands you a gift to take with you. Look at the gift. See what it is. Feel it. Know it. Tell your loved one how you feel about the gift.

Now ask your guide to show you if the quarrel and this meeting ended your relationship with your lover or spouse in that life experience.

See if the quarrel and this meeting cemented the relationship and permitted you to reestablish your love and live out your lives together.

Understand clearly how this quarrel and this meeting— and its aftermath—have affected your present-life interaction with your lover or your spouse.

Understand clearly why you have come together again to learn a lesson left unlearned, to complete work left unfinished, to evolve together once more—for better or worse.

14

Discovering Who Your Child Was

Your child may be one of those who talks about past lives while clinging to the sides of the playpen. There is little question that babies are often aware of memories of prior-life experiences. We have experienced remarkable statements from our own children, and we have heard dozens of parents share similar accounts with us.

We believe that within your soul, your higher self, there exists the wealth of information received from many past lifetimes. Soul contact permits you access to the collected wisdom, knowledge, and love experiences your soul has gathered since the beginning of its physical time.

There are many discovery games you and your family might play with your child that will assist you in determining who your child was in a former lifetime. By this time you are fully aware that we are not encouraging you to come up with a King Arthur, a Cleopatra, or a Napoleon sitting there watching cartoons on Saturday morning television. Regardless of whatever past-life information you might obtain about your child, once again we stress that the value of the following exercises and techniques truly lies in making contact with the higher self and in permitting that wider perspective to help your child lead his or her current life more completely.

Whenever you begin a program of developing greater awareness within your child—or anyone, for that matter—it is always best to begin with various "tuning-in" exercises. We are certain that once you have followed the ones we suggest, you can probably come up with some of your own.

In everyday life, reality is held fast within rigid boundaries of time, space, and matter so that we may devote ourselves to the daily task of obtaining sustenance for our bodies through various forms of work. These confining walls of reality simply must be removed if one is to attain greater awareness. There is no need to be concerned about whether or not the borders of Earth plane reality will return after you have stretched your consciousness. The harsh requirements of the world and of life will see to it that the walls return all too soon.

It would take years of steady and faithful practice, unflagging spiritual discipline, and meditation techiques of the highest degree to enable you to remove the strictly structured walls of Earth plane reality. The adept who can accomplish such a task while in the physical body will attain the highest of all awareness on this planet.

Everyone in the family may benefit from playing the discovery games we are about to describe and from participating in the awareness exercises we are about to share.

Try the following as a kind of "warm-up" exercise. Have family members gather small objects from throughout the household without letting one another see what has been collected. Blindfolds, pads, and pens should be ready at the meeting place—let us say in the living room.

When the objects have been gathered and everyone has his or her blindfold on, each participant should exchange objects with another member of the family. Each player should then "tune in" and receive as much information as possible about the object he or she now holds.

Aid the younger children by asking them what very first impressions, what "pictures" come to mind. Perhaps the children will see a scene that depicts the day and the place the object was found or acquired. Maybe there will be a mental picture of the person who first found or bought the object. A thought may cross their minds that describes the emotions of the object's owner.

When no further information appears to be forthcoming, ask the players to remove their blindfolds and quietly jot down their impressions.

There should be no talking to disturb others who may still be receiving or writing down their impressions.

Children who cannot write yet should be told to sit quietly and to think about what they saw and felt. They should be the first called upon to recite their impressions.

When each player has finished writing or thinking about the object's impressions, a group sharing should take place. Since the items gathered were all household possessions, the adults present should be able to verify whatever correct images were received about each object.

A variation on this game is to have each member take his or her turn leaving the room while the others select one object on which to concentrate.

Have those members remaining attempt to send their thoughts of the item to the player who is absent.

The member who has left the room should then return, recite all the impressions he or she has received about the object, and seek to identify the item concentrated upon by the group.

Explain to the players that in order to send impressions to another, they should first gather mentally all their energies within, concentrate on that single object alone, and picture it before they seek to broadcast a description of it. Then they should let loose of the image and thought and clear their minds. If they hold on to the image, they have not sent it.

Explain to them that this is the difference between reading thoughts and receiving them. So-called mind readers "read" thoughts contained in the mind of another.

Receivers are capable of snatching thoughts from the psychic atmosphere or of receiving images sent directly to them. Point out to your players that the latter is the greater and most useful skill to acquire, for it aids immensely in one's creativity and awareness.

Another simple attunement exercise begins by instructing your players to collect pictures from magazines. These pictures may be of scenery, athletic events, people—anything.

When the pictures have been gathered, tell the players to place blindfolds over their eyes while you shuffle the illustrations.

Have each player pick a picture on which to concentrate. Instruct him or her to tune in to the picture selected and to spend three to five minutes receiving impressions.

When the receiving time has been completed, instruct the members to turn the pictures facedown then remove their blindfolds. Now allot them about three minutes or so to jot down on a pad all the information they have received about the picture.

After each player has finished writing down all that came to him or her, tell each member to turn the picture over and compare what s/he has written with the picture. If any of your players are too young to read or write, have these children recite their impressions aloud *before* turning their pictures over. The results of this game can be very exciting.

In another variation of the above exercise, each participant takes a turn at being a sender to the group. Place the sender at a table away from the group, who turn their backs to him/her. Spread the pictures before the sender, bidding him or her to select one on which to concentrate. When the sender has made the selection, turn the other pictures facedown to avoid psychic "spillover."

Remind the sender to gather mental energies, think only of the image s/he selected, then send it to the group—let it go! Suggest that the group of receivers sit quietly with their eyes closed, better to facilitate their reception by shutting out all other images that might try to creep into the untrained mind.

This awareness game, like the previous one, may also be played by having each participant take a turn in leaving the room while those remaining select a picture on which to concentrate. In this variation, of course, the group sends their impressions to a single receiver, who jots down or remembers all the images and thoughts s/he receives. Compare the impression s/he received with the picture on which the group has been concentrating.

You will soon determine who in your little discovery group is the greatest natural sender and who is the most proficient receiver. After this has been ascertained the sender should practice receiving and the receiver should improve his or her ability to send. Each of them should strive for a more balanced awareness, and each of the other members of the group should seek the same goal. In time you will have developed an extremely talented group of psychically aware and spiritually balanced individuals.

The next awareness and discovery game we share with you is one that must be described with a bit of caution. This game is played with unknowing participants whom you might encounter in your day-to-day existence. The exercise has many variations, but basically the purpose of the game is to cause another to perform a harmless act.

It is of the utmost importance that you make the act a harmless one, a positive one. Remember always that good begets good in the world of energy, the law of karma. A negative act will be visited equally upon the perpetrator. A negative act always boomerangs upon the sender.

We must remember that the mind is like a television set that has myriad channels available to it. There is no possibility of being unwillingly controlled by another's thoughts unless you are already tuned in to that person's "channel." A harmless suggestion, such as to scratch or rub an area of the body, is not screened by one's values or morals. Acts other than these unthinking, normal body responses, acts that would require one's evaluating whether they are right or wrong, cannot be sent by anyone, no matter how adept, unless the receiver is already tuned in to the possibility of performing such an act.

Let us say that a sender who has long practiced the skills of mind energy saw a man standing in front of a large plate glass window. Let us further suppose that our sender is very angry, struggling with hostility that has become uncontrollable, and he transmits the suggestion that the man in front of the window should shatter the glass. Unless that man is operating with an open channel to hatred and anger, he will not pick up the transmission.

Of course, all this implies responsibility for our thoughts, for if that man in front of the window were open to hostility at that time, he just might heed the transmission and smash the glass. Truly we must be cautious about the thoughts that we transmit to others. If our transmission should be responsible for someone's carrying out a negative act, we in the world of vibrations, will be held jointly responsible for the action. We reap that which we sow, and we and the receiver would pay the loss equivalent to the deed performed.

We would be well advised to send out loving thoughts so that we may be more likely to influence men and women to do acts for the betterment of humankind. If those who are tuned in to positive thoughts receive our transmission of positive actions, then again, both we and the receiver will gain from the good vibrations of the beautiful work accomplished.

It is best that your group first practice on willing subjects. Ask one of the players to leave the discovery circle and instruct those remaining to decide upon the action on which to focus. It might be to rub or to scratch or to touch a particular area of the body.

If the subject has a habit of pulling the tip of his nose when he talks or when he is under tension, it would be no challenge to concentrate on his performance of that act. But if the group were to concentrate on the subject's tugging at an earlobe, actually varying a habitual behavior pattern, that could be significant.

When the subject is brought back into the room, he is seated in the center of the group. Each member of the circle concentrates on causing that particular area of the subject's body to itch, let us say. Whether it is the scalp, the shoulder, the knee, or the foot, each member focuses on having the subject scratch or rub the spot that itches.

This exercise is better performed when the group members close their eyes so that they do not inadvertently give the selected area away by continually glancing at it. You, the monitor, will be able to tell them when they have scored. When the target area has been scratched, select another player to leave the room and to take a turn.

When you enlarge upon this exercise, you have the entire world in which to have fun. This game can make a long, tedious ride on public transportation a great deal livelier. This exercise can do much to shorten the minutes wasted while standing in line at the supermarket or the theater. At the same time that you are eliminating boredom you are also sharpening your sending abilities.

Little concrete information is known about the forces and energies that you and your children are utilizing in the many above-described activities.

They defy gravity.

They make a mockery of time and space.

They pass easily and unnoticed through walls and bodies.

They can effect both animate and inanimate things.

They can truly change your life.

Learn how to use them positively, constructively, in order to benefit you in your life. Nothing is impossible to you.

Storytelling games can prompt the mind to remember past lives. "Let's tell stories" comprises an excellent method by which parents may come to learn more about who their child was. In the guise of simple storytelling the parents may gain a great deal of valuable information about past lives that are directly affecting the child's present or future-life experience.

Remember, though, just as in the case of an adult who fabricates a fanciful tale, the child will most likely include elements from a combination of television programs, motion pictures, and stories that have been previously told to her. The younger the child, the less liable you are to have overlap from everyday experiences and other cultural input, but you must still be cautious of feedback from television programs absorbed by the child's conscious and unconscious mind.

If you have a talkative child, it is wise to record this story. When children feel at ease, most of them become "hams" and delight in the feeling of importance when parents think enough of their stories to record them on the cassette machine. If your child is shy, however, and you see that the microphone inhibits her, you can still record the story in secret. Playing the recording at a later time will usually delight the shyest of children, for they marvel at the sound of their own voices and enjoy the personal attention.

The parent who subsequently analyzes the child's story must be extremely attentive to detail. As he or she reviews the tale, the parent must skillfully unravel it, removing from consideration those aspects of the story that the child could have learned from other sources. The parent must keep in mind the age of the child, the child's level of awareness, degree of perceptiveness, the ability to comprehend adult situations. Storytelling is an informative game to play, for you will gain perspective on your child's world-view and the impressions he or she might have of other people.

It is best not to make the child aware of what you are really trying to accomplish. Place your child at ease in every conceivable way so that his or her thoughts may flow freely from the subconscious mind. This is why it may be best to have only one parent play the storytelling game with the child. Children sometimes feel intimidated when attempting to please both of the most important people in their lives.

Another way to insure that the child is not disturbed in any way is to make certain that his or her bodily needs have been taken care of before the game begins. As most parents well know, little ones will squirm for several minutes before admitting they must relieve themselves. Therefore, see that the child has a comfortably full stomach, has recently used the toilet, and isn't thirsty before beginning.

One should make certain that the child is dressed comfortably in loose clothing, with nothing binding.

Distractions must be minimized. Advise both your friends and your children's friends that you are not to be disturbed for at least an hour, then disconnect the phone.

It is frequently observed that a child, upon relating a past-life memory, seems greatly relieved and frequently does not wish to rediscuss it when later prompted to do so. In certain cases it appears that the child has honestly forgotten the memory after relating it. However, there are always exceptions. Some children delight in retelling the story and are able to embellish it with further details left out on the first telling.

After a productive game of storytelling the parent should immediately begin transcribing and unraveling the tale, sorting fact from the fantasy of everyday existence. Pare the story down, underlining the areas not known to be current experiences, crossing out lightly those areas you feel the child has gathered from this life.

Put the story aside and return to it with a fresher outlook after a couple of days. See if the underlined areas could have conceivably come into your child's mind from his or her present experiences. The last phase is then ready to be employed.

Use a relaxation technique, relaxing your child from toes to head. Retell the story after s/he is in an altered state of consciousness, totally immovable, as if asleep. Remember to advise your child throughout the muscle-relaxing technique that the body is to sleep while the mind remains awake and aware of your voice.

It is up to you whether you wish your child to be able to

speak with you throughout the past-life experience, or whether you wish him or her to experience the past-life suggestions and share impressions with you upon awakening. We suggest you try both methods to see which gives you better results.

After the child is completely in an altered state of consciousness, retell the child's story and permit the child to add to the scene he or she will then imagine.

Some parents have found that merely relaxing the child from toe to head and asking him or her to see a former life led in another place and time will obtain similar results. Whatever method you employ, the story revealed will be fascinating.

Here is a suggested list of subjects to ask the child about while he or she is in an altered state of consciousness.

Inquire as to the country; the approximate time; a very important historical event that has just occurred about which the world will one day know, such as a war, plague, famine, earthquake, or flood.

Name, sex, and age.

The clothing worn by men, women, and children.

The various implements used in farming, mining, building, creating.

The kitchen utensils employed in the households.

The beliefs and behavior patterns of the people.

What his or her mother, father, loved ones looked like.

The famous and important individuals living during that time.

The most important person in the town, city, state, country.

How did he or she die? What happened?

Remember, the soul translates into the child's own language and speaks frequently in symbols. However, on occasion a highly psychic child or a trained child can recall various sentences spoken in another language. This is wonderful proof for those able to obtain it, and it is best to have a recorder running at all times for a permanent testimony.

Try to make the storytelling game as enjoyable as possible. A child who is having fun will be more alert and communicative.

If you are informed about historical events and you have some knowledge of the period of time your child is describing, name people known to be living and events that are occurring, and ask questions about them. Also, one good technique is to ask your child to sing a song he or she sang while rocking a child to sleep or while performing a lengthy task. Many subjects recall simple lyrics and songs that in a past life they repeated many times over.

Remember to tell your child to look into a mirror, a piece of polished metal, or a clear pool of water in order to see an image, so s/he can describe his or her face. Ask the child if he or she looks like any person, famous or otherwise, that he or she knows in the present existence. This device is helpful in obtaining an accurate description.

A notepad and pen kept nearby will permit your child to write his or her name, or the name of the country or to jot a phrase in the language used then.

Such questions as, "Did you know your present mommy then? Daddy then? Brothers and sisters then? Grandma, grandpa then? Who were they then?" are apt to reveal many things.

It is undoubtedly obvious that all the above questions are usable for any age. So is the following technique. We call it, "On the Wings of a Snow-White Dove" in memory of a well-known song whose lyrics seem most appropriate as well.

On the Wings of a Snow-White Dove

First use a relaxation technique, beginning with the feet and continuing up to the head and face, relaxing and causing every part of the body to fall asleep...

You are in a beautiful country setting. Everything here is so peaceful, so beautiful and you are relaxed. Velvet flowers in a myriad of colors surround you. Luxurious trees encircle you with a healthy, vibrant green. A clear sky is above you, spotted with puffy white clouds. As you lie in the midst of all this spendor, you are resting and taking deep, comfortable breaths. Birds in colorful array flit from tree to tree, whistling melodiously.

A flock of beautiful, loving doves descends near you. They seem happy, engaged in loving interplay.

One of the flock, a large, glowing white dove, steps toward you, gracefully coming nearer. As it comes closer, it looks into your eyes. You can tell it is not an ordinary dove, but a special one. It comes so close, it rubs against your cheek with the deepest of love.

As the dove touches you, you feel the inner you, your spirit, begin to tug and to slide from your physical body. It is a lovely, wonderful, free feeling and you permit it to slip out.

You easily slip from your shell, and as if by magic you can control the size of your energy transmission. You make yourself smaller and you see the white dove before you squat low so that you may mount it.

You climb aboard its neck as if riding a beautiful pony. You delicately fluff the feathers of the dove's neck and enjoy its luxuriant softness. The dove spreads it wings, and within a moment it is aloft, flying.

The dove ascends higher, higher—higher still. You enjoy the thrill of flying with it.

Faster it goes. The wind blows through your hair. You enjoy the breath of fresh air available to you at this height.

Glancing down, you see the beautiful countryside below you, stretched out as if a green blanket has been poured over hill and dale. Trees beneath you appear as tiny bushes, and a stream threads its way as if it were a shiny blue ribbon.

Before you is a cloud, a puffy white cloud of soft texture, dense and thick with water. Droplets of water mixed with brilliant sunshine reflect through the cloud, causing each drop to act as a prism. Every color of the rainbow is before you. Rose, yellow, green, blue, purple, and violet. These are beautiful and pure colors and vibrations, and you can feel them as you see them.

You desire to pass through these beautiful colors, knowing that they will increase your mental awareness and strengthen your soul contact. You pass through them, feeling and seeing yourself and the dove, upon whose back you are riding, bathed in each and every color.

Rose. Feel the color rose surround you, wash over you. You are rising in vibration, increasing your mental awareness, contacting your soul.

Yellow. Feel yellow all around you. You are bathed in yellow and your dove is glowing yellow. You are elevating your vibration, increasing your awareness and contact with your soul.

Green. Healthy, living green is all around you. You and your dove are bathed in this living green. It is raising your vibrations, increasing your awareness, helping you to contact your soul.

Blue. Feel and see blue all around you. You and your dove are bathed in blue. You feel your vibrations raised; your contact with your soul increased.

Now see before you *purple,* majestic, royal purple. You and your dove are bathed in purple, and you feel the higher vibrations of the color purple enter your being. You feel also an increased contact with your higher self, your soul.

And now, *ultraviolet,* the highest frequency of all prismatic colors, the highest vibration available. This vibration of unconditional love now passes over you, surrounds you and your dove, fills you both completely. You feel love. You vibrate with unconditional love for all living things. Love as you've never experienced it before fills you as you enter the dimension of your soul.

You feel your soul. The unconditional love vibration places you in contact with your higher self, your soul. You merge with it and feel glorious! You feel alive, free, enriched with a wealth of love, wisdom, and knowledge available to you.

Feel the love here. Feel the knowledge contained here. Feel all the wisdom it has gathered throughout its experiences in time. Feel the soul. Rejoice in contact with the soul. Vow from this time forward to maintain contact with your higher self, your soul. Permit it to enter your life, your everyday activities.

You are beyond time and beyond space. You no longer care about your physical attachments in the way you once did. You see Earth's physical relationships and all who reside upon the planet in a new light, in an awakened awareness. This place is your true inner space, and you are one with it.

You can feel that this place is in direct contact with the Source. Feel the love, feel the energy here. You are floating as one, merged with energy from the Source. You love the peace here. You will return to this place time and time again, whenever the need arises. Whenever the desire comes to be near the Source for strength, for life, for pure love, you will come here.

Now as you drift in reverie, surrounded by your higher self, your soul, you find here knowledge of all the lifetimes it has lived.

You concentrate on a particular lifetime you desire to explore, whether it is in direct relationship to the lifetime you are living at present on the Earth, or whether it is in direct contact with certain people about whom you desire to know further. You have records here of all the lifetimes your soul has ever lived. All information is available to you from this place. Be it your past, your present understanding, or your future possibilities, all are found here in this place. Come here when you desire to know all.

At this point your subject is capable of perceiving all he or she desires to know. Ask and it shall be given.

After a period of ten to twelve minutes remind your child that all things that are for his or her good and gaining will be remembered.

The dove spreads its beautiful, white, glowing wings; and again you are aloft. You are bathed again with all the beautiful colors—ultraviolet, purple, blue, green, yellow, and rose. You feel peaceful, harmonious, happy. You understand more than you ever dreamed was possible. You will remember for all time that which you have come to know, and you will visit this place you've been again and again.

Return now to Earth. Awaken joyful, aware, and loving. Awaken with greater resolve than ever before to permit your soul to reflect through you throughout your life.

The imagery of the snow-white dove can make anyone feel at peace, at one, enriched, and full of unconditional love for all living things. The benefits are boundless. The Universe and all its dimensions are yours to give to your child in his or her spiritual quest.

Seeing Who You Were and Tuning In

These two exercises are recommended for children beyond the age of twelve. Younger children might become a little frightened by the images they would see. Of course, these two methods can be used by adults as well.

Sit comfortably in front of a mirror set at eye level. A red light should be at hand, with a switch you can easily snap on and off. Place yourself in a receptive state while seated in a dark room with your hand resting on the light switch.

Quiet yourself, relax your body, and breathe deeply, comfortably for several minutes. Tell yourself that only the hand on the switch will be able to move easily.

Stare at the darkened mirror before you. Think of your higher self. Think of your soul. Concentrate on your soul's energy entering you as you breathe deeply, staring at the dark mirror. Wait several minutes, then ask to see the face of your soul. Flash the light on and off and see your soul's image.

After several minutes, ask to see the face worn by your soul in a former life that is directly related to you now. Ask to see the face of that person before you.

Flash the light on and off several times, staring in the mirror while thinking of your soul. Ask to know something of that person, the country, the time, the life, while flashing the light on and off.

Now, with the image before you, firmly fixed in your mind, lie down nearby. Relax your entire body from toe to head. Relax yourself completely. Think of the face that was before you in the mirror—and whatever else you received. Breathe deeper and deeper, centering your thoughts on only these images. Do this for at least five to eight minutes—resting, relaxing, floating, drifting into the images before you.

The very same exercise just described works as well with a minor alteration. Instead of a flashing red light, place a small candle nearby while you sit in a darkened room staring at your image in a mirror. Quiet yourself in the same manner as before, request soul contact and ask to see the face of your soul, and then ask to see the former life led and to learn all you can while viewing it. Relax yourself and meditate as before on the images given you.

A Tip for Easy Imagining

As an aid in visualization, cut a ping-pong ball in half with a finely serrated knife and file down any rough edges. Tape the edges of the two halves to your eyes or the eyes of your child, covering them entirely.

Now seat yourself, your child, or your subject before any source of bright light, natural or artificial. With the eyes now held open, quiet the self and relax every part of the body, beginning with the feet and moving up to the head. Soon images will begin to form, and no one need ever teach you or your child how to imagine again.

This visualization aid is especially effective for children just beginning to explore awareness techniques and for adults who have a difficult time visualizing. This aid encourages the beginner by "priming and pump" with "instant images." Suggestion quickly takes over and converts the light into meaningful images.

15

Dream Teachings and Symbol Language

A young man from Texas once came to us with an unusual recurrent dream. It seems that he would often find himself on a barren stretch of desert awaiting the arrival of *something* unknown that filled him with apprehension. He would hear a roaring noise, then he would see what appeared to be a huge, black bowling ball rolling toward him.

It was at this point that he would usually awaken, fearfully pulling back the sheets and covers, sitting up, relieved to find it was only a dream.

"I've had this dream several times in the past four weeks," Jeff told us. "I know that this dream is trying to tell me something, but I just can't seem to break through and understand the symbolism of it all."

In our presession discussion with Jeff it became readily apparent to us that he was a very spiritually evolved young man. He was in the practice of keeping dream diaries, and he was well read in metaphysics.

"Nothing has come to me in meditation, either," Jeff explained. "I'm really at a loss to understand this dream or to know why it seems to disturb me so. I've got a hunch, though, that it has something to do with past lives."

First we led Jeff through an analytical process designed to help us understand his internal symbolism, then we relaxed him in preparation for leading him through the awareness techniques that would explore his past-lives—especially any that might provide a clue to the big black bowling ball. We asked Jeff's guide to show him a past life that he needed most to know about for his own good.

Jeff was seeing himself in ancient Rome. He was a bookkeeper for a wealthy government official, and to his dismay he had recently discovered that his employer was cheating hundreds of business associates. Worse, he had knowledge that his employer's corrupt practices exploited his servants, slaves, and employees to the extent that many had lost their lives.

In that past-life memory Jeff saw himself summoning his courage and speaking out against the deceit of the government official. He heard himself denouncing the man in public gathering places. He relived the moments of crisis when he was finally effective in gaining the ears of certain powerful men who in turn demanded that the employer defend himself against the charges of corruption.

The story did not have a happy ending, however. The entity who was a facet of Jeff's soul in that prior-life experience had only a fleeting moment of glory. The government official was too wealthy, too influential to be greatly affected by Jeff's accusations. Witnesses were bought off or eliminated, and soon Jeff heard himself being sentenced to death in the arena for having brought false witness against his employer.

Now Jeff clearly recognized the original environment for his recurring dream. He was not in a desert, but in the sands of an arena. He now recognized the strange roaring sound as that of the mobs gathering in the Circus Maximus for their daily pleasure of seeing some poor wretch spill blood.

As things came into focus, Jeff saw that the "big black bowling ball" was in reality a black bull, a gigantic horned beast that was preparing to charge him.

At this point we were careful to keep Jeff emotionally

detached from the scene he was reliving so that he would experience no trauma, so that he would feel no pain.

The bull was pawing the sand, snorting its rage at the men who were prodding it with long spears, bellowing in pain as the metallic points drew blood.

Jeff stood alone in the arena. He had been given a short wooden sword as a mockery of defense. There was no place to run. There was nowhere to hide. The angry bull would soon charge him, bunting him with its massive head, impaling him with its long horns.

Jeff gained the awareness that he had died in that lifetime because he had spoken out for truth and justice. He had spoken out against corruption and he had been sentenced to death for his act of courage.

When we brought Jeff back to full consciousness from the relaxed state to which we had guided him, he had been given the insight he had sought. For about a month he had been aware of a business situation in which he felt his firm had not conducted itself properly. He had become convinced that his firm had unknowingly cheated another firm. He had the facts, but he had been reluctant to confront his partners with the information. His conscience told him that he must alert his associates to the error, but he found himself unable even to bring the matter up at their twice-weekly meetings.

That was when the dreams began. A memory from a past life was surfacing to inhibit Jeff in making the correct and the ethical decision. A facet of Jeff's psyche was remembering a time when he had died for speaking out against the business tactics of an employer. The crisis was being acted out nightly in the arena of Jeff's mind, and the continued playback of ignoble death in front of screaming mobs kept him from a confrontation with his partners.

We pointed out to Jeff that matters had changed considerably. In this life Jeff was no longer a bookkeeper in the employ of an unscrupulous official. In his present-life experience he was the peer of those whom he must confront.

At the same time he was not facing corrupt and

exploitative men. He was dealing with his own associates who had made what might well be an honest error.

The sooner he explained the true facts of the transaction to his partners, the less "face" his firm would lose with the other firm and the less awkward the whole matter would become. No one would sentence him to death at the horns of a great black bull in his present lifetime.

There are many techniques anyone can use with the dream state to gain knowledge about past lives. Upon going to bed at night, after you have become fully relaxed and are lying still with your eyes closed, suggest to yourself that sometime during the next day you will have a revelatory image and/or thought about an important past life that is directly affecting your present-life experience.

The suggestion should state that sometime during the following twenty-four-hour period an image, thought, or emotion somehow linked to a previous lifetime that is directly influencing your present interaction with others will "pop" into your mind. It is even more effective if you suggest that the past-life link be an image that can aid you in dealing with a specific problem. Suggest that the images provide you with a solution to the problem.

For example, if you are distraught over your mate's seeking the company of others, you might make the following suggestion to your subconscious before falling asleep: "What event in another life experience is causing me to suffer the pain I know now, the dilemma I now feel, when my mate is unfaithful to me? Tomorrow, sometime during the day, an image or remembrance of the past life that is directly related to my current problem will be revealed to me."

Sometimes an implantation might have to be repeated several times in order to be completely productive.

Consider the case of Laura. For two years she had gradually been becoming the sole companion of her children, serving more and more as both mother and father to them since her husband, Jim, seemed to have less and less time for his family.

During the day, Laura would do the cooking, baking, feeding—seeing to the traditionally maternal responsibilities for her three kids. Toward evening she would don sweatshirt and jeans, and romp and play ball and roughhouse physically with her children, thereby providing them with a father image.

Although Jim was a good provider, he appeared to be deliberatly detached from his children. He seemed to have erected a wall around himself to prevent invasion by his kids.

Laura was quick to give Jim credit for having given her a more than adequate home, but she was beginning to find their marriage an imbalanced one. The children, too, longed for their father's physical, as well as financial, presence. Both Laura and the children were willing to give up some of their material benefits in exchange for more contact with their husband and father.

Laura was familiar with the subconscious implantation method, so she decided to try it in order to gain some answers regarding her relationship with Jim.

Upon going to bed, she relaxed her entire body. Just moments before sleep came she made the affirmation: "Tomorrow, sometime during the day an image will come to me that will help me to remember a past-life experience that is responsible for Jim's being more concerned with our material needs than with our emotional requirements. I will see, know, and remember the reason why we are now suffering this absence in our lives."

As an additional psychological stimulus Laura would imagine herself and the children in a room filled with great luxuries. In this image Jim always stood outside, never entering, just placing objects of material worth into the room.

It took Laura just three days to discover the answer to Jim's emotional aloofness. The thoughts and images came to her as she was wiping fingerprints from the refrigerator.

It is interesting to note that these flashes of memory and understanding most frequently occur when we are performing mundane tasks, when we are doing robotlike duties that require no mental effort. These insights often burst into our consciousness when we are sweeping the floor, brushing our teeth, driving the car, dusting the furniture, watering the lawn, and so forth.

Laura seemed to be instantly removed from her kitchen and her refrigerator, and to be watching the bent figure of a woman sorrowing beside the weeping form of her husband. She felt within her heart that she was that woman, that Jim was that husband.

The two tragic figures were crouching over the bodies of two dead children. A third child was crying piteously in a corner of a darkened room illuminated only by the light of a flickering candle. An old man was coughing, spitting up blood. An old woman was leaning weakly against a wall.

In her sudden burst of memory Laura was aware of her husband, "Jim," crying out loud: "My children. My parents. I have loved them so. I have put so much of my life into them. And now the Lord is punishing me for my idolatry of family by sending this terrible plague to take them from me."

"It is God's will, my husband," she heard the woman saying.

"It is God's punishment for my having loved my family so much, for having placed my love for them above my love for Him!" the man wailed mournfully.

Just as quickly as the emotional vision had come, it slipped away, leaving Laura with her cleaning cloth in her motionless hand.

She was left with the knowledge that in another lifetime she and Jim had been married and had produced two children. Jim had worshiped his children and he had been a dutiful son to his parents. Then a plague—judging from the clothing she had seen, perhaps a plague that had occurred during Europe's Middle Ages—had come to take the lives of the children and the parents he had held so dear.

Laura could now better understand the detachment Jim had been displaying toward the children. A past-life memory of having lost the children he loved so much had caused him to be cautious about investing his emotions in his present-life offspring.

Laura knew now that she might aid Jim in his emotional deprivation.

She would help him to focus on the joy of fulfilling the present. She would help him realize that nothing on the Earth plane lasts forever. She would help him understand that one must enjoy each day to the fullest. She would guide him in recognizing the truth that the soul is eternal and that we come together in many lifetimes with those whom we love. She would point out that his children hungered for his presence and that he should not deny either himself or his kids time with one another.

Later, in discussing certain aspects of reincarnation with Jim, we learned some interesting facts about his background that may have triggered the past-life memory within his psyche. Jim had been raised primarily by his grandparents. His mother and father were two obsessively career-minded people who provided him with luxuries and gifts but deprived him of their love. He had learned to accept the material expression of their responsibility to him and to survive without emotional expression of their love.

Rather than reincarnation in Jim's case, one might also argue that he was simply enacting a pattern of luxury over love that had been enforced upon him by his present-life parents. Laura's subconscious mind may have been well aware of this pattern and created a past-life scenario which would help her better to understand or to accept Jim's detachment toward the children. On one level of mind, then, Laura knew why Jim was so aloof, but by casting the situation in a past life she was provided with images that would help her to deal with the problem and give her another framework in which to present the matter to her husband.

What is really important is that Laura was given an answer to Jim's studied detachment that enabled her to confront him with the sad evidence that their family unit was being destroyed by his aloofness and remoteness. Jim could respond without taking personal offense to the rationale that a past-life aspect of his soul had already suffered through the problem. He could permit a past life to identify an anxiety he may only have been aware of on a subconscious level.

The end result—subsequent happiness for the children of Laura and Jim—is the important matter. Whether Jim's personality alteration was due to psychological factors or past-life recall is really immaterial.

Few people utilize a very useful tool of the mind that Francie calls, "the mood inducer." The discovery of this techique came in 1948 when she was in the sixth grade.

A substitute teacher, Mrs. Jones, told Francie's class that there was no excuse for tardiness. Mrs. Jones said that she herself awakened on time every morning without the use of an alarm clock. She instructed the children merely to tell themselves the very hour they need to awaken only a few moments before dropping off to sleep. She advised them to be certain to repeat the mental instruction several times.

Francie tried this method the following morning and woke up minutes before the alarm went off. She found that not only did she awaken at the self-appointed time, but she awakened far more relaxed and refreshed than when she had been startled out of a deep sleep by the noisy clanging of her clock.

Francie has used this method throughout her life with amazing success, enlarging upon it as the perimeters of her world expanded.

"In other words, if my morning's schedule was expected to be particularly demanding, filled with business matters, I would program myself the night before so that I would awaken feeling quick, alert, precise. On the mornings when I knew I must be creative, I would preprogram myself the evening before to be filled with an awareness of the Universe and boundless creativity.

"I soon discovered that I could control this mental mechanism throughout the day, so that I might better perform in the manner that others demanded of me—and that I expected of myself.

"All I needed to do was to find a place of solitude, such as an empty rest room. I would elevate my feet, totally relax my body for several minutes, then program myself for a particular hour. Perhaps a certain meeting had been scheduled or a television talk show or an important business conference—I could always be refreshed and ready with the desired mental outlook.

"When a particular day had been very hectic and I found myself drained, unable to perform for an evening's commitment, I would go off by myself, relax the muscles of my body, then preprogram myself to become alive, aware, alert with a positive demeanor at the necessary hour. Surely enough, when that hour arrived I could feel my programming button go off and my body fill with renewed vitality and energy.

"I have taught personnel managers and various executives whose job is to find the most efficient person for a particular job how to tune in to those individuals being considered. I have demonstrated techniques of preprogramming to them so they are open and receptive to everything they must consider on all levels before reading applications, before scanning personnel records or arranging interviews. Their results were nothing short of miraculous. They marveled at how accurate their mental assessments became.

"I have maintained sporadic contact with many individuals employing this preprogramming method, and I am continuously amazed at the inventive ways many have used it.

"Those who are athletically-minded preprogram themselves for peak endurance; dancers, musicians, artists, and actors use it to achieve their greatest performances. Designers, writers, and directors gear themselves for their finest creativity. The variety of uses is up to the individual, whether it be for a certain meditation time or for responding sexually to a mate. Preprogram yourself for success!"

With practice you will find yourself able to preprogram your dream state.

Through dream studies conducted at various laboratories throughout the world, it has been discovered that we all dream nightly, whether we remember it or not. In fact, most of us have three to five dreams per night, each lasting anywhere from five to twenty minutes on the average. Those people who for some extraordinary reason do not dream or have their dream state repeatedly interrupted, hallucinate. They dream while awake.

The dream state is the time when the subconscious mind is permitted to talk symbolically with the conscious mind, advising it, readying it, soothing it, or taking it to task for some failing.

However, with the preprogramming technique, you can dream about a past life that your soul has lived that can aid you in understanding a particular problem you are now facing. Or you can preprogram yourself to dream of a past life in which you were involved with a certain individual you presently know. In this way you can discover the circumstances surrounding your soul's former relationship with that individual and add to the awareness of that person.

With this method you can utilize at least one of your dream periods each night for research into your past lives. Whatever you wish to discover—a particular talent achieved in a former lifetime, a certain understanding not previously accomplished, or the pure pleasure of activating a deeper level of awareness—preprogramming can achieve it.

A paraplegic we know who has an incessant desire to travel uses this very method for enjoying all the countries where his soul has lived. He even interacts at times with those people he feels he is meeting there. In his dreams he finds that he is not encumbered by his speech impediment and he is able to walk. On these visits he delights in skipping, running, and jumping.

Practice makes perfect, as with any skill, but pre-programming your dreams is one of the easiest techniques of awareness to master.

During the dream state we are receptive to any thought that our mind might wish to receive. The dream and the trancelike state offer particularly good times for past-life memories to surface.

During wakefulness we construct shells and defense mechanisms of varying degrees around ourselves. It may well be that these shells are necessary to protect us from the many assaults of daily living, but these same protective shields often block contact with higher awareness.

We heartily recommend setting aside time for daily meditation to permit you to reach a state of consciousness that will help you to receive awareness. We also earnestly suggest altered states of consciousness to assist you in reaching out from yourself. We feel the dream state can provide the seeker with one of the most productive areas in which to receive memories of past lives and teachings from higher levels of intelligence.

In *The Star People* Francie channeled information on how to develop the ability to understand individual symbol language that we want to share with the reader at this point.

Keep a notepad on your bedside table, together with a small file box of cards tabbed from "A" to "Z". Each night before you retire, date the notepad.

When you awaken, record your dream. Underline the subject matter.

For instance, let us say that you were purchasing new shoes in your dream, because the shoes you were presently wearing were damaged. You tried on many pairs of shoes before choosing a pair that felt comfortable. Now understand the subject matter, *damaged shoes exchanged for new shoes*. Think of what "shoes" may represent.

Your feet are your foundation. They permit you to walk comfortably wherever you choose to go.

Remember you tried on many shoes until you found a pair that was comfortable. Trying on several pairs may indicate that you will have to try many paths. You should change to a new path on which you feel more comfortable, because the way you are now walking is damaging to your awareness (remember the *damaged* shoes in your dream).

On an index card, you should write: *"Shoes."* Beneath the topic write, *Damaged shoes exchanged for new shoes:* I should change my way of going for another, more comfortable way."

Now file this card under "S" for shoes.

Each dream has major subject matter. Nearly all events symbolically received can be filed by the particular subject, its meaning, and how it directly relates to your personal experience.

I do not wish to influence your own personal dream symbology, but here are a few subjects most often dreamed of by sensitive men and women and the meanings which I have come to recognize in a large number of consultations:

Trees: People, living lifeforms, whose outstretched arms reach to the Source of energy. Low branches indicate people who are easy to reach, to whom you can easily relate. Trees with high branches represent those people who are difficult to reach.

Mountain: Master Teacher or wisdom from the Source.

Water: Creative energy. The water's condition, muddy clear, will indicate to you how you are using your creative energy.

Food: That which we take into ourselves daily, such as the attitudes of those around us.

Attacking Animals: Hostile people or problems.

Birds: Messages of awareness flying toward you from beyond.

Doors: New ways open to you.

The manner in which the subject matter normally relates to you is usually the measure of understanding its meaning.

If you should dream that you have mud all around you, you'll best understand this image by realizing how you would react—and what state of affairs you would be in—if mud really were all around you. You might feel that there was no path out of the dilemma. Therefore, in the waking state, you would have to seek a way out of circumstances which your dream showed as "mud" surrounding you.

If you should dream of being all alone in a boat in the middle of a large body of water, you may feel that in the waking state you are helpless to use properly the creative energy that is all around you. Give of your creative energies during the day, and you will find your life becoming more positive and productive.

After even a few nights of productive dreaming, you will find your file box beginning to fill up with your dream symbols and their subjective meaning to you. You will be able to flip to any subject matter and recall what it means in your life.

After a period of about a month, you will have memorized your symbolic dream language, and you will have become more aware of everything about you. You will know much more clearly *what* you must do. You will have received a glimpse of what is in store for you in your *future*.

16

The Timeless Realm Where Visions Live

For some, experience is the best teacher; but those who have received vision teachings feel these are the most thorough way of gaining awareness. Though the words "vision teachings" may seem self-explanatory, the complete understanding of the entire concept of visions aids the seeker in attaining the desired result. Knowing what you will encounter once you embark on the quest of awareness helps at the beginning of your journey.

Here, then, is a step-by-step description, so you might know the anatomy of a vision teaching. When you are given a vision teaching, you are taken out of your body and lifted away from the physical dimensions of Earth. You feel more alive, more complete, and as if you are fully protected. You feel freer than you have ever felt before.

With your arms outstretched at your sides you soar vertically into space, higher and higher. The wind blows past you, tossing your hair. Your heart is filled with awe and love. Never before have you experienced such a wondrously beautiful feeling. Space is dark, but multitudes of colored lights sparkle around you. Stars, planets, nebulae, galaxies being born—the Milky Way moves soundlessly by.

You continue soaring higher and higher until you stop quite gently, as if standing in space. It is as though you hang suspended. There is a quietness in this stark realm that prepares you to open up to what you anticipate is forthcoming.

Here in this timeless realm you will receive visions, living diagrams, thought awareness. You can be shown the past and explore the previous lives that your soul has lived on Earth or in other dimensions of reality. You can understand more thoroughly your present situation, your mission to Earth. You can even receive the future. Sometimes diagrams appear that symbolically explain the great mysteries of existence—the questions humankind has asked since intelligent thought first formed in the more illumined corners of the brain.

You have the ability to enter a dimension that operates on a higher vibration, where unconditional love, wisdom, and knowledge exist and can be given to you. With practice you can transcend to the space beyond the physical realm and lead a more meaningful and productive life.

Some teachings will be given to you in words, without an accompanying vision; yet the words create thoughts that permit the mind to imagine the new information almost as thoroughly as if a diagram accompanied it.

When you permit yourself to enter an altered state of consciousness, you must want to receive awareness, to receive a vision teaching. You must desire to be taught, so that a greater understanding of many things may then be yours. This desire must be uppermost in your heart and mind.

You will be transported to a beautiful realm where a magnificent, colorful panaroma of living diagrams, teachings of awareness, or past-life experiences will be given to you. While you are in this realm, unconditional love will permeate your entire being. It is in this dimension that angels, masters, and guides will visibly or invisibly interact with you, share with you, teach you all that you desire to know.

What you will see here cannot be contained. It must be shared and it must not be permitted to stagnate. What you receive here and see here, *must* be shared with others.

In the giving, you will more fully understand what you have received, and you will be able to describe it and relay it more easily. You will also receive anew. You must give to receive, just as you must give any energy before you can receive the same energy afresh, anew. You must give love, wisdom, and knowledge before you will be able to receive them again anew.

When you receive such a vision, you will be totally happy for having had the contact occur, but you will also experience a deep sadness for your precious time that elapsed before such communication was made. Both of these emotions will be felt at the very same time. You will open your mouth to wail, to mourn, to laugh, and to shout for joy—all at the same time. This mixture of feelings accompanies contact with higher intelligences and vision teachings. There will remain no doubt that what you have witnessed has been from beyond, from the Source of all that is.

The receiving of a teaching vision comes when you are meditating, when your mind is quiet. Prayer is not meditation. Prayer is speaking, asking. Meditation is receiving, listening, waiting. If any mundane thought enters your mind, gently push it away. Never shove an intruding thought away from you. Instead, tell it that you will think of it later...and gently, very gently, ease it from your mind.

With the eyes closed most people see vague outlines of images or swirls. With practice the images will become clearer, focused, with colors coming in and going out. Soon the colors will remain and become vivid—then all will be clear. As always, practice makes perfect!

Meditation is an art form wherein you receive the creative energy awaiting you. Soon you will become a part of the scene of the image, and you will experience it for a time.

Next, you will find yourself freely flying through space

to a particular destination that has been selected by your higher self, your soul, or perhaps by your angelic guide, master, or teacher. When you reach this place, you will receive many awarenesses. You will feel the air move over your body, through your hair. You will feel freer than you have ever imagined. You will free yourself from the material world to which you have always been attached and step into the true reality of all that is.

Your vision teaching will come to you in a matter of minutes—ten at the very most, rarely more—though you may feel as though an hour has passed. This is a truth that appears universal, for in that domain, in the altered states of consciousness, there exists no sensation of time as we know it.

When you receive your vision teaching, a feeling of "knowing" will envelop you. You will feel that you have always known this awareness, and you will have an inner belief that what you have received is truth. You will feel it vibrate in your heart and in your stomach, as both will vibrate together, a heart and a gut-level feeling. No one will be able to shake you from your belief in your teaching vision.

When you tell others of your teaching, you will be able to speak beyond what you were consciously aware of at the time you received the vision. This is due to your having not only absorbed the frequencies of higher awareness that accompanied the vision teaching, but also because you learned more than you were consciously aware of. You have thereby been elevated in your vibrational awareness. You will be able to comprehend more than you could have understood before the vision teaching was ever received.

By telling others, you will become even more aware of the entire truth than when you first envisioned it, for you can now perceive it from many sides, and gain different perspectives. By giving you receive in greater abundance.

Vision teachings are parts of a living, vibrational truth that is composed of many facets of varying levels. Depending on your personal awareness, you will see the level of truth nearest your own understanding.

As you grow in awareness, you will perceive deeper levels of that very same truth, as if you are ascending a beautiful, terraced landscape or a mountain that permits you to view the world around you more clearly as you climb higher and higher. As you elevate your vibrations, rising in awareness, you will be able to achieve the highest level of consciousness and, thereby, one day see all of the very same truth.

All truth teachings appear as separate visions to our understanding, awareness, and perception. Yet they are not separate at all. They are connected one to the other, as are the images on a great tapestry.

The more aware you become, the more your vision grows with you in depth and complexity until your awareness and higher vibration permit you to see it in its entirety. It is in this way that you discover the one truth, the Source of it all. It is in this way that you discover God.

The Cosmic Vision Quest

To embark successfully on this vision quest it is necessary that you place your subject—or yourself—in as deep a level of consciousness as possible by using one of the relaxation methods described elsewhere in this book. Again we advise you either to solicit the aid of a trusted friend or family member to read the following suggestions in a deliberate and thoughtful manner, or to prerecord the material yourself on a cassette tape so that you may serve as your own guru. If you wish, you may simply place yourself in as deep a level of relaxation as possible and contemplate each of the visions that we have suggested.

You are visualizing yourself standing or sitting on a peaceful beach at night. You listen to the sound of the ocean waves gently touching the shore.

You look up at the night sky, splashed with a million stars. You can see the sky from horizon to horizon. You feel in harmony with Earth and sky. And as you look upward at the stars, you ask yourself deep, meaningful questions:

What is the true meaning of life?

Why did I really come to Earth?

What is my true mission on Earth?

How can I make better sense of my life?

Is there anyone out there beyond the stars?

Is it possible to make contact with an intelligence from out there?

As you think these questions or speak them aloud at the stars, you begin to notice a particularly brilliant flashing star high overhead. As you watch it, it seems to be moving toward you. It seems to be lowering itself to you.

Now you see that it is not a star at all. It is a beautifully glowing object.

You feel no fear, only expectation. You feel secure in the love of the Universe. You know that your guide is near you.

You feel unconditional love as the object with the sparkling, swirling lights lowers itself near you. You know that it is a vehicle that has come to take you to levels of higher awareness.

A door is opening in the side of the light vehicle. You look inside and see that it is lined with plush, soft velvet. You know that it is safe. You know that it is comfortable. And it glows within the golden light of protection, the light of unconditional love from the very heart of the Universe.

Step inside, settle back against the soft, comfortable cushions. The door silently closes and you know that the vehicle now will take you to those higher levels of consciousness. You are completely comfortable, relaxed, soothed; but you know that you are being taken higher and higher, to total awareness.

You look out a small window at your side and you see Earth below you becoming smaller and smaller as you rise higher and higher.

Colors seem to be moving around you. Stars seem to be moving around you.

You feel love, pure, unconditional love all around you. You are being taken to a dimension of higher consciousness. You are being taken to a vibration of a finer, more highly realized awareness.

You know that you are safe. You know that some benevolent force is taking you to the timeless realm where visions live.

You know that you will be safely returned to Earth once you have been to the in-between Universe, the in-between dimension where teaching visions await you.

Colors swirl around you. Stars swirl around you. You are moving across the galaxy.

You are traveling higher and higher, higher into the very soul of the Universe. You know that you will receive meaningful teaching visions when you reach that timeless realm where visions live.

And now your light vehicle has come to a stop. You look out your window and see that you have stopped before a beautiful golden door, a door that seems to be suspended in space.

You know that when you step through the beautiful golden door, you will find yourself in the timeless realm where visions await you.

You know that you will have the ability to perceive and to comprehend meaningful teaching visions—visions designed especially to provide you with deep and profound insights and understandings.

When you step through the golden door, you will enter a dimension that exists on a higher vibration...and your mind will be totally attuned to that frequency. You will have the ability to receive clear and revelatory visions. You will receive the answers to questions you have asked for so long, so very, very long.

When you step through that golden door, you will enter a realm where magnificent colorful panoramas of living diagrams and teachings of awareness will be given to you. Unconditional love will permeate your entire being. Angels, guides, master teachers will interact with you, share with you, teach you.

And now the golden door is beginning to open. A panel in your light vehicle is sliding back, permitting you to leave its interior, allowing you to step through the golden door.

You know that you are protected; you know that you are guided; you know that you are loved. You step from your light vehicle and you move inside the golden door.

As you step inside, you know that you have the ability to perceive and to understand profound teaching visions.

As you step inside, the first sight that awaits you is the view of a marvelous crystal transformer, a crystal tube that is a very special vehicle that will take you into the plane of ultimate awareness where the teaching visions await you.

You will know that when you enter this tube and move higher into the timeless realm, some teachings may be given to you in words, without an accompanying vision. These will be insights, thought forms of encapsuled awareness. Other teachings may be given to you in visual thought forms, living diagrams.

Stand now before the crystal tube.

Stand now before this very special transforming vehicle that will take you to that exact place where visions live, where only love exists, where you will have the ability to receive your vision teachings.

A panel in the side of the crystal tube, the crystal transformer, is sliding back to permit you to enter.

You know that you want to receive the answers to so many questions, answers your vision teachings will provide.

Step inside, step inside the crystal tube and feel unconditional love all around you. Lie back against the soft lining of the tube. Make yourself totally comfortable. The panel slides softly, silently closed, and you begin to move to the special place where visions live.

You are moving *out*...you are moving *out* now...or is it really in?

Stars seem to sparkle around you. Stars seem to move around you.

And now it seems as though the crystal transformer, the crystal tube, has disappeared and you are hanging suspended in space, totally protected by the golden light of unconditional love from the very heart of the Universe. And you have the ability to receive your first teaching vision.

The first living diagram appears, sent to you by the Source of all that is...This living diagram explains to you, the true nature of the soul...the true nature of the soul and what really happens to the spirit after the physical death of the body.

You are seeing now your true relationship to your soul...your soul's relationship to your guides...to God...to the Universe.

You are seeing yourself making the physical transition of death in a past life.

You see and understand what truly happens to the spirit at the moment of physical death. (Pause for two minutes to permit impressions to form.)

Now your second teaching vision is beginning to manifest itself. This second living diagram explains to you, the true nature of other intelligences in the Universe.

You see alien lifeforms.

You are focusing on a planet, a city, a people, a culture—all of which are alien to Earth.

You are seeing an alien people. You are seeing their history, their customs, their belief structures, their technology. (Pause for two minutes.)

Your third teaching vision appears. Your third living diagram begins to form. This third vision explains to you your most important past life, your Karmic Counterpart.

This is the past-life experience that has been most influential on your present-life experience.

You will be shown, and you will understand, the importance of this previous-life experience in terms of your soul's evolution to the Source of all that is.

You will see details that will help you to understand your present-life experience. You will see details that will help you to see why you are the way you are...why things have progressed the way they have progressed.

You will see who came with you into this life...and why. (Pause for two minutes.)

Your fourth living teaching vision is showing you scenes from future time. You are being shown the face of the Earth in the new age.

You are seeing this planet as it will look after any Earth changes have taken place.

You are being shown changes in society...art...politics ...economics...clothing styles.

You are being shown the skylines of cities. You will not be shocked by anything that you may see...even if cities are underground...even if new coastlines have been formed ...even if new mountain ranges have appeared...even if new people walk among us. You will see and you will understand.

From the vantage point of looking backward from the future, you will now see where the safe places will be.

Look at a map of the United States...Canada...wherever you wish. The safe places will glow with golden energy. See and understand where the safe places will be.

And as you gaze into the future, you have the ability now to see an important future-life expression of your soul.

You are being shown now an important future-life experience that your soul will live on Earth...or elsewhere.

You have the ability to see yourself and to know what you are wearing...the color of your hair and eyes...whether you are male or female—or androgynous.

You see your environment. Your domestic life-support systems.

And you see who is with you from your present-life experience or from any previous-life experience. (Pause for two minutes.)

And now your fifth living diagram appears. You will now receive insights as to your true mission on Earth...why you really came to this planet in the first place.

You will be shown, and you will understand, why and when you first chose to put on the fleshly clothes of Earth.

You will see why and when you first chose to enter the karmic laws that bind this planet.

You will see and you will understand what it is that you are to accomplish in your soul's evolution in this place of learning. (Pause for two minutes.)

And now your crystal transformer has reappeared. Once again it appears to be solid around you.

It has come to take you back to Earth time, back to human time, back to present time, back to your present-life experience.

You will remember all that you need to know for your good and your gaining.

You will be strengthened to face the challenges and the learning experiences of your life.

And know this: The more you share your visions and your teachings, the more your understanding of them will grow.

You are now awakening, surrounded by light and by love, by pure, unconditional love. You feel very, very good in mind, body, and spirit. You feel better than you have felt in weeks, months, years.

You will awaken fully at the count of five.

17

Experiencing Ancient Lands

Visiting an ancient land or any land while in an altered state of consciousness is a wonderful, exciting adventure. You actually feel that you are there. And while in the altered state your senses are keener, sharper than they are in the waking state, thus adding to the sensual pleasures you will experience during your journey.

All those psychic pilgrims who have traveled before you reported that they could feel as well as see. In other words, the sight of flowers before you will permit you to feel their velvety softness. You can feel as well as see the entire countryside. In the altered state flowers smell sweeter than usual, and all colors are perceived more vividly than in the waking state. The wind blows through your hair; the grass feels cushiony; pebbles are a bit rough underfoot; spring water is cool, soothing and wet; the sun comfortably warms you; and all your wishes can be fulfilled. You will not be encumbered by gravity. You can enjoy running faster than normal, leaping with giant bounds, flying with childlike enthusiasm.

By tapping the realm of eternal time you can venture anywhere you've longed to see, at any time in history.

You can see Earth when it slumbered, before any life existed. You can watch the miracle of creation as life awakens over all the Earth.

You can explore the lands of darkest Africa, South America, the Orient, and Europe. You can watch as ancient civilizations rise and fall. You can see Greece—the Acropolis, Socrates; Rome in all its glory, Caesar and his mighty legions; Egypt, the builder of the pyramids; Palestine, Moses, Jerusalem, Jesus; Europe in all its splendor; America as it stretches forth across the plains.

Or you can even travel beyond, to the Moon, Venus, all the planets, the Milky Way, Sirius, the entire Universe.

All these enchanting places can be visited; all of these adventures await you. "Nothing shall be impossible unto you." And you can do all this at your own convenience, in the privacy of your own home.

Careful preparation for your altered states experience will assure you of a marvelous inner voyage. Choose the place or places you wish to visit and the times you've desired to see. Next, select books that are descriptive of these areas and eras, and record all the scenes that appeal to you, all the experiences in which you wish to partake, the people you would like to meet. Record as much about the place you have selected as you would like to experience. For variety create a montage of vacation plans that will involve many times and many places on this Earth—and even beyond. When you are in an altered state of consciousness, totally relaxed with your mind free to roam, you will see, feel, experience every place and every time suggested.

Specially selected background music befitting the place you wish to visit aids your visualization, for we have all been trained through motion pictures to have music accompany visual scenes.

You are now ready to venture forth. There are three methods of travel. The first has many advantages, and it requires the use of a tape player. With this method you merely play your tape whenever you desire to venture forth. First record the relaxing exercise of your choice, then read your notes of the scenes you wish to see, the people you desire to meet, and play the selected background music.

The second method of travel is to have a trusted friend help you, acting as your guide, reading the relaxing exercise, then the scenario notes, while background music is played softly.

And for those who have strong wills and determination, you can travel by thought. Place yourself in an altered state, relax your entire body, then mentally direct yourself to visit the places you desire to see. With practice, your mind will become more compliant, your will stronger.

In this method, instead of visualizing yourself walking from one place to another, merely *think* where you want to be and you will be transported by thought to that spot. Thought travel takes a little practice, for we are used to placing one foot in front of the other to move along. All you need is discipline and patience. You need not panic if you feel you cannot move. Just think of returning home and waking up, and you will—for your thoughts become your actions.

As a further aid to help you in creating your own trip to an ancient land, you may use the following visit as a guideline. Throughout the world many people who are regressed identify somehow with ancient Egypt in at least one past life. Therefore, we feel the visit to Egypt would have the widest range of appeal.

First, select the muscle-relaxing exercise of your choice, then you are ready to travel.

A Visit to Ancient Egypt

You are relaxed, completely and totally relaxed. Your body is asleep while your mind is alert.

Up ahead you see an area in the middle of a mighty forest, and it beckons to you. It awaits your presence. You feel yourself drawn to it, and you walk toward it.

It is a quiet space, a grassy circle bordered with low plants. You stand in the midst of this lovely spot and enjoy the calmness here. Not even a breeze stirs the surrounding trees.

You notice that there are many paths that lead from this place, and many different kinds of trees line each path. Before you a twisted oak, beautifully gnarled, flanks the northward path; to the left a statuesque birch gleams white in the afternoon sun.

You must think now of Egypt. The Egypt that was, the Egypt that will always be.

A slight breeze stirs the limbs of a mighty tree to your right. Its rustling leaves beckon you to come. The sweet, strong aroma of fresh eucalyptus is wafted to your nostrils, filling your lungs. You breathe deeply, slowly, enjoying its cleansing aroma.

You approach the path that is lined with these green, majestic giants. You know deep within your heart that this path leads to your beloved land, Egypt, ancient Egypt.

The path is grassy, and it is soft to walk upon. It is wide enough to permit easy movement between the huge trees.

You are fittingly garbed in a white garment and sandals proper for the time and the occasion.

You glance far ahead, up the grassy path. You notice how the beautiful, thick trees stand guard as silent sentries, making your journey safe.

You think of Egypt, ancient Egypt with every step you take. Egypt with its many splendors. Its pyramids at Giza, the sphinx, Memphis, the sacred bull at the Apis sanctuary.

Somewhere deep in your memories you recall the smell of the warm, spicy winds that come from deepest Africa. You remember them gently nudging your boat as you traveled with the current up the Nile.

Now you are on the Nile, in a safe, strong boat. You are paddling to shore and you begin to glide between riverbanks lined with thorny acacia trees, sweeping willows, and towering sycamores.

Here is some of the most fertile land of Egypt. An almost unbroken string of villages and towns, home to half a million people, border the shaded riverbanks. Ripening stands of wheat and barley lie between lines of tall, green palms. The ground is reddish brown, soft, rich, fertile silt.

You watch as women come to fill large striped jars with water to take home, balancing them on their heads. Herds of cattle come to the river's edge for a drink.

Your eyes feast on the beautiful pyramids that dot the desert. The tawny sphinx crouches low on the brown desert sand.

The desert lies farther back now, at the foot of steep limestone hills that shine white in the noonday sun but cast dark, long shadows over the valley at sunset, when the sky glows pink. Great ponds abound here. They adjoin the river, and they are filled with tall reeds, papyrus, and blue and white lotuses.

You watch from a safe distance as hippos and crocodiles move lazily in the hot sun. Paddling easily to shore, you begin to glide along the narrow riverbank, lined with thorny acacias, sweeping willows, and towering sycamores.

The sky grows dark now. Glancing up, you see why. Swarms of geese, ibis, and other waterfowl are flying overhead. The sky is filled with them.

Flamingos stalk proudly in every shallow of water. Looking out over the tall reeds, you watch skimming swallows perform majestically overhead.

You feel as though you remember being here as a youth. The tattered, colorful wings of a beautiful fuzzy moth flutter by as you pull into a narrow inlet and tie your boat.

Before you is a large village that sprawls on the edge of the great desert. Its walls are made of branches, mud, and stones. You can see its beautiful temple rising high above the sand-colored wall, glistening in the sunlight so all eyes may gaze upon it. You feel you can remember meeting, and knowing some of the people who live there as you approach it.

As you enter the large village, you notice that the gates bear colored pennants. The guards permit your entry.

In the path of the shadow of the temple stands the royal mansion. A large, half-buried dwelling of mud-brick guarded by sentinels is before you. Farther to your right are small adobe huts and other homes of wooden frame.

You wave to the friendly villagers, who smile and warmly greet you. You seem to recognize some of them as you slowly pass by. Others approach you, talking to you. Their words are easily understood. Somehow you can mentally translate them. And they understand you as well.

As you talk with them you gaze beyond, to the edge of the village, where a scattering of umbrella-shaped acacia trees and low desert shrubs lie. Far in the distance you see hunters returning home.

You bid the villagers farewell and walk toward the temple to your left. Your steps quicken as you approach its golden doors. Tonight you will attend the royal celebration. All people of importance will be there. They will gather to celebrate with the gods.

The gods and the people rejoice when the Nile is about to rise, for many bellies will be filled. The granaries will be stocked to the brim. All Egypt will benefit. Crops will be plentiful, beer and wine will flow. Healthy babies will be born.

The temple doors are before you. Golden images of the gods greeting the priesthood are carved upon them. Pushing the doors open, you enter.

The sweet, musty fragrance from the blending of many spices permeates the air. Standing before you is the beautiful statue of Nut, the mother of Heaven. To your right sits the lion-headed goddess Sekhmet crowned with the disc of the sun. The laws of cause and effect, karma, are believed to be in her care. Next to her sits the cat god, Bast, never a normal "Miu." To your left stands Anubis, the jackal-headed god, guardian of the other side of Heaven, the underworld. Beside him sit Osiris and Isis, rulers of the underworld.

It is well known over all Egypt that Heaven is above Earth as well as below; that Heaven is as one mighty sea upon which the stars, sun, and moon travel before descending into the underworld, the other side of Heaven. The movement of the celestial bodies constitutes a nightly pageant of reincarnation, of death and rebirth, and all peoples believe it. All hope to visit the underworld when they pass through the doorway of death to be reborn in the east, as are the stars, sun, and moon.

You light some incense, say a prayer, and glance up as several priests and priestesses approach you.

"It is time to go to the royal mansion. The celebration will soon begin," they call out to you, quickly passing by.

You stand before the Sacred Eye, Udjat, with six perfect parts, and ask that your *own* six parts be made as whole and as perfect. You ask that your sight, touch, hearing, taste, smell, and intuition be made whole, perfect, and balanced. You promise to use them for only positive endeavors throughout your life. In this way, living positively, you, too, will be born in the stars. You bid all farewell and you rush to attend the royal celebration.

Leaving the royal temple you cross its path and approach the doors to the mansion. You display a ring that serves as your ticket of admission. You notice as you enter the mansion how high the windows are and how they let in only a small ray of sunlight for illumination. It is cool inside, for the thick walls of the half-buried dwelling keep out the desert heat.

Murals are everywhere. You admire the brilliantly colored birds and flowers painted in shades of green, blue, and orange. Elaborate palm columns decorated in gleaming gold support the ceiling. Woven reed mats cover the floors, and servants rush back and forth as they prepare for the night's festivities.

The sounds of the orchestra that you see practicing in a large corner of the next room can now be heard. They are rehearsing for the many guests soon to come. Oil lamps are lighted around the room, casting a warm, eerie glow over all.

You are led to join the royalty in their walled-in garden near a cool, blue pool, under the leafy branches of tamarisk trees. The king and queen appear quite elegant. Both are bewigged and decorated in shiny garments and wearing elaborate cosmetics. You are greatly impressed with how warmly and lovingly they speak to you and to one another.

They discuss with you and the others gathered around the importance of serving Earth's people, as do all of Egypt's gods. They tell you that all service is to be performed in the name of the Source, in the name of all that is. In this way the Source of all things is truly loved and honored.

The prince and princess, a boy and girl both under seven, run in to greet their parents. The children desire to spend the early evening playing with their mother and father before they go to sleep. The king and queen act as any other young, proud parents, kissing, cuddling, and tickling their little ones. Mere frowns, which transform the queen's and king's smiling faces, are all that is needed to reprimand a naughty little one.

While the royal family is playing, you delight in being able to speak personally with the high priest. He motions for you to join him as he sits by the pool. You hear him say what is expected of one who becomes a servant of the priesthood, a priest or priestess.

He tells you, "What is within must always be reflected without. Be in total balance and harmony. Your thoughts must be balanced by your actions. Truth must be sought as if it is your food, for it *is* your spiritual food. In this way, one attains many awarenesses.

"Whatever the visions or the teachings that you receive while contacting the other side, they must never be changed by you, for all given is holy. Chaotic forces, negativity, will be visited on those who do alter them.

"All who serve the Source must learn to give unconditional, nonjudgmental love to all—yes, all living things. This is so that you may be a worthy vessel in which to carry divine teachings, to be an instrument of God.

"You must spread these awarenesses. Feed others who seek you out, who are spiritually hungry, so they, too, may join with their souls, their doubles, who waits for them in the stars."

The priest tells you that many who choose to serve the Source are taught in the temple, in their dreams, and in their daily meditations. In these ways they sometimes learn of coming disasters, so as to prepare the people who follow and to make their own way safe. These servants are children of God, of goodness, of the Source.

A servant hands you an alabaster goblet of delicious red wine and a tasty delicacy of figs and honey freshly baked into a soft wheat roll. You eat and drink. It is delicious.

The music is haunting and melodious to you, and you can hear the sound of oboes, lyres, lutes, double flutes, and drums.

The voices of other guests can now be heard, and the royal children are kissed by their parents and led away by a servant. The royal couple ask that you join them in greeting the other guests gathered in the main room.

The dancers have begun and you can see them swaying back and forth as you walk down the long hall toward the room. The dancers are stamping and kicking their feet in rhythm to their clappers. They dance in unison, weaving in and out through the crowd. They pass near you, smiling as you enter the room. They are attractive people and their movements are very hypnotic.

You have finished eating and a servant moistens and dries your hand without your asking. The other initiates and the high priest have already entered the room. As you enter, many call out to you and you greet them. You feel great joy, and they come to you, hugging and kissing you.

As soon as you are seated, the acrobats enter. Large and small, they climb on one another, balancing themselves precariously, first on one hand, then the other. Finished, they tumble merrily from the room.

Next the wrestlers enter. Many cheer over their favorite's maneuvers. The armlock and the flip-over are standard holds and throws. No one is ever hurt. All is for fun.

Some guests appear to have drunk too much wine, for their loudness betrays them. But you notice the members of the priesthood, the servants of the Source, do not drink to excess. They are balanced in all they do.

All men and women who are gathered enjoy the innocent fun, for infidelity and adultery are not tolerated. Unfaithfulness is frowned upon, even by the commoners.

You enjoy yourself and speak with many men and women. Your time is spent most pleasurably. (Pause here for approximately two minutes.)

And now a loud bell has been struck in the nearby temple, and its sounds echo into the party. The guests begin to leave, bidding good-byes and safe journeys to one another. Many come to you, personally bidding you farewell. You quickly bow and give thanks and many blessings to the royal couple, their servants, and others who welcomed you so warmly. Then you leave the mansion.

You will remember and cherish this visit forever. You step outside and breathe the cool night air as you glance out over the moonlight-flooded valley. The waxing moon hangs silent in the velvet black sky. The stars stand as crystal sentries, guarding over all.

One star shines brighter than all the others, and you feel within that this is *your* star. You vow then to shine forth as a star, throughout all your life, reflecting your soul in all that you do.

You feel complete, within as well as without, and you ask to be made as whole as Udjat, the Sacred Eye. You feel all of your senses becoming whole, balanced, and complete, as if for the first time. Your senses are complete to the fullest degree possible.

On the count of six all of your senses will be awake, totally, completely (1) your sense of smell, (2) your touch, (3) your sight, (4) your taste, (5) your hearing, (6) your intuition. Awaken complete, whole, reflecting your soul, happy and positive.

AWAKEN!

18

Becoming a Spiritual Alchemist

We are more things than we can imagine. More processes take place within us than we know. We are all multidimensional beings, and we have the ability to learn a psychospiritual discipline—true magic—so that we may control a marvelous universal energy that will permit us to achieve self-mastery and to work miracles.

The alchemist's true goal was not simply the transmutation of base metals into gold. That process served as a metaphor for the transmutation of the alchemist himself into a higher substance.

For thousands of years certain spiritually adept people have known that an aspect of their multidimensional selves can interact with an as yet unidentified energy, an unknown force, and cause the mind to influence matter. The Hindus call this force *Prana;* the Chinese, *Chi;* and Japanese, *Ki;* the Hawaiian Kahunas called it *Mana;* the plains Indians, *Wakan;* the Nordic people, *Wodan.* Christians call it the *Holy Spirit.* All cultures at one time or another have sensed an unknown energy underlying all paranormal phenomena and constituting an essential part of all life on the planet. The exciting thing is that the conduit for the X-Force, the *Mana,* the *Prana,* whatever you choose to call it, appears to be the human being him/herself.

In speaking of the X-Force, Dr. William Tiller has observed that we are dealing with an energy field completely different from those known to conventional science. A biological transformation seems to be taking place in humankind. New energies appear to be circulating on our planet. As some level of the Universe we are all interconnected to each other and to other organisms and to other levels of consciousness.

In this exercise you will be guided to where you may link up with this unknown energy and permit your own psyche to become a conduit for this remarkable force that sustains the planet.

Place yourself in a deep level of consciousness by utilizing one of the relaxation methods previously described in this book or a technique with which you have success. Either prerecord the following suggestions or have a friend read them to you in a deliberate and thoughtful manner. If you prefer, of course, you may simply place yourself into as deep a state of relaxation as possible and contemplate each of the suggestions we have provided.

Visualize the color blue moving over your body as if it were a blanket-like aura. Feel it moving over your feet, soothing them. Feel it moving over your legs, relaxing them. Feel it moving over your stomach, your chest, your arms, your neck—soothing them, relaxing them.

Now as you make a hood of the blue cover, feel the blue permeating your psyche so it uses the X-Force to utilize telepathy, clairvoyance, psychokinesis, prophecy, and healing. Once you have done this, visualize yourself bringing the blue-colored aura over your head.

You are now sitting or lying totally secure in your blue-colored cover. You are very receptive, very aware. You feel attuned with higher consciousness. You feel prepared to explore deep, deep within you, deep, deep, within you...

You are seeing memory patterns before you. They may be your memories of a past-life experience. They may be other memories. It does not matter. You are seeing them before you now.

The memories are taking you to a faraway place in a faraway time.

As you are moving back in time, you are aware that what modern people call a primitive, magical language is actually a symbol system that represents universal forces. What modern people label magic is a means of relating to certain energies that few people today are able to perceive, much less master.

The technological compulsion that drives modern humans to conquer nature has reduced our sensitivity to these energies. You feel saddened as you realize that modern people too often feel comfortable only when dealing with destructive forces.

As you move back in time, you become aware that the Universe is conscious only to conscious humankind.

As you move back in time, you are remembering a lifetime in which you knew, from your personal experience, that there exists on Earth an unknown energy that can be manipulated through the mind.

As you move back in time, you are remembering a prior existence when you heard the great magus Eliphas Levi say: "There exists an agent which is natural and divine, material and spiritual, a universal plastic mediator, a common receptacle of the vibrations of motion and the images of form, a fluid and a force, which may be called in some way the Imagination of Nature...The existence of this force is the Great Arcanum of Practical Magick."

As you move back in time, you are remembering a lifetime in which you traveled to Egypt, Egypt of the second century before the birth of Jesus.

You are remembering that lifetime now. You are remembering that you heard certain scholars tell of an ancient manuscript that was found in a column of an Egyptian temple.

You heard a scholar say that this book told of events that occurred at the beginning of time, when great beings communicated certain secrets to initiated adepts.

You have heard it said that this incredible primeval

revelation is being taught in secret to a few select adepts in hidden rooms in the pyramids. The objects of these alchemical teachings are health and longevity, the manipulation of physical matter, and the production of the elixir of immortality.

See yourself now walking a street in Egypt of that time. There is a full moon, and you can see everything around you very clearly.

You are approaching a home with a courtyard. It is the home of a very old and wise teacher who can lead you to a secret room in a pyramid and give you the initiation that will make you alchemically adept.

Take a moment to experience fully your emotions as you walk up the path to the home. Feel your expectations deeply.

Look at the walled home of the teacher. What plants grow near the walls? What is there about the immediate area that most captures your attention?

Now you are at the front gate. Be aware of your inner thoughts and feelings as you knock. Feel your knuckles strike the wooden planks.

The gates open as if by themselves and you see the dancing flames of a great open fire that burns in the center of the courtyard. You are able to see a man dressed in robes sitting near the fire. You know that it is the master teacher.

As you approach the fire, a student steps forward and places more wood upon it. As the flames dance higher, you are able to see the teacher very clearly.

Become totally aware of him. See his clothes, his body, his face, his eyes, his mouth, the way he holds his hands.

You have brought a present to him so he might recognize you as a seeker of wisdom.

Take your present out of the leather bag in which you have carried it. See what it is that you hand the master teacher. See his reaction to the gift.

The teacher gestures to you that you should follow him. He has approved of you as one who will receive initiation.

You are now in a tunnel. You are being led to a secret room within one of the great pyramids.

Experience fully your emotions as you walk silently through the tunnel. Feel deeply your expectations. See the torches set into the walls. Be aware of any aromas, any sounds.

Now you are in a great room. Look around you slowly. You see statues, golden statues of Osiris, Horus, Isis, Bast. What other statues do you see?

Look at the walls. See the paintings of Nut, Selket, Sekhmet. See the hieroglyphics.

Are there other paintings that seem strangely out of place? What are those paintings? What else do you see written or painted on the walls?

The teacher is showing you a great crystal that is supported on a golden tripod. He says that it is the philosopher's stone. He advises you to obtain a crystal to wear around your neck to assist your transmutation of self.

As you stare into the crystal, the teacher tells you that he will now bestow upon you the initiation. He says that it will be for your particular needs alone. The teacher will tell you what you need to know from him. He will tell you what you need to know to continue your quest.

Observe him closely. He may transmit this knowledge with a facial expression alone. He may transmit this knowledge with a gesture of the hands or a movement of the body. Or he may transmit this knowledge at some length with carefully selected words. He may even show you an object or a symbol. However he transmits the knowledge, it will be for your good and your gaining. He is transmitting this knowledge...now...(Pause for approximately two minutes to receive impressions.)

Whatever the master teacher has told you, he has bestowed this gift upon you, for you are moving through the purple mists of time to seek wisdom from another great master.

You have heard it said that there exist certain great alchemists who become immortals, wandering for centuries upon Earth, concealing their condition of immortality and revealing themselves to only a few fellow alchemists. You are now approaching the forest cottage of such an alchemist. He is one who has achieved enormous fame as a wizard. He has shaped kingdoms and tutored kings.

You are walking the forest trail without fear, for the wizard has sent a knight in armor to guide you. It is night, there is a full moon, and the trail is easy to see.

As you approach the cottage, what do you most notice about the house and the outbuildings?

Is there a garden? Do trees grow near the main building? Take a moment to know the wizard's environment.

The wizard is said to be able to answer any questions about the unknown energy that might be put to him. You are pleased that you have received an invitation to visit this wise old man.

The knight walks you to the open door of the cottage, then steps aside so that you may enter alone.

As you enter the cottage, you see the crackling flames of a great open fireplace. A man dressed in robes sits near the fire, stirring a huge iron kettle with a large wooden ladle. You know he is the wizard.

As he turns to face you, you see his features clearly in the firelight. Become totally aware of him. See his clothes, his body, his face, his eyes, his mouth, the way he moves his hands.

He gestures to you that you should be seated. He hands you a cup of his favorite tea and you savor it gratefully. Taste the tea in your mouth. It is a very special tea, seasoned with herbs.

The wizard nods to you, indicating that you may now ask your question about how you might best develop control of the X-Force.

As you ask how best to develop telepathy, clairvoyance, knowledge of past lives, knowledge of future events, knowledge of the talent of healing, knowledge of control of physical matter, see how carefully he listens to you. See how thoughtfully he considers your question.

He will now tell you what method will be best for you. Observe him closely. He may answer you with a facial expression alone. He may answer with a gesture of the body. He may answer you at some length with carefully selected words. He may show you some object or a symbol. However he answers, he will tell you what you need to know to develop your spiritual abilities. However he answers, he will tell you what you need to know for your good and your gaining. He is answering the question...now...(Pause for approximately two minutes to receive impressions.)

The knight appears and tells you that you must now leave the wizard.

As you are saying good-bye, the immortal one reaches in his robe and brings forth a leather bag. He tells you that he has a very special gift for you. He wants you to take the object with you. He opens the leather bag and hands you the gift.

Look at it. See what it is. Take the gift. Feel it. Know it. Tell the wizard how you feel about him and his gift.

Now the purple mist of time is once again swirling around you. You are once more enjoying the alchemists' mastery of cosmic time and human time.

You are now standing before a very wise man in a vast and cluttered laboratory. Your inner guidance tells you that you now exist in the time sequence that is Europe in the sixteenth century. The man before you is a physician known as Paracelsus, and alchemist, a thinker, and a great man. Listen to what he tells you.

He says that nature does not produce anything that is perfect in itself; humankind must bring everything to perfection. It is the alchemist who fulfills nature. As an example, he says that God did not create objects made of iron. God created the metal, which must be enjoined with Vulcan, the god of fire, in order to fashion useful items.

Nothing has been created in its final state. Everything is first created in its primary state. It is the alchemist who must bring the fire of creativity to make art.

Alchemy is the art that makes the impure into the pure

through fire. It can separate the useful from the useless and transmute it into its final substance and its ultimate essence.

Only the soul lives eternally. The soul endures while the body decays, just as a seed must rot if it is to bear fruit.

Decay is the midwife of great things. It brings about the birth and rebirth of forms a thousand times improved. This is the highest and greatest mystery of God.

There is nothing in Heaven or in Earth that is not also in humankind.

In men and women is God, who is also in Heaven; and all the forces of Heaven operate likewise in us. Where else can Heaven be discovered if not in us?

Honor all people equally, for what is in you is in all.

In men and women the ability to practice all crafts and arts is innate, but not all those arts have been awakened. Those things that are to become manifest in man must first be awakened. Because all potentialities are inherent in humankind, what you awaken in them will come forth; the rest remains unawakened, absorbed in sleep.

Human beings are born to be awake, not to be asleep.

Now, O ye who seek wisdom of self and knowledge of the unknown energy, receive a great awakening! Receive a great understanding of how best you may use the X-Force in your life. Receive this wisdom and understanding—now!

19

Receiving Illumination

Throughout the centuries, inspired men and women have sought the transfer of an energy, a thought, a spirit, or a power from an infinite intelligence to their own finite, human intelligence. Some people call this energy the *Chi*, the *Mana*, the *Prana*, the Holy Spirit, or the X-Force. We have also named it the divine fire.

We believe that the divine fire employs a spiritual-psychic mechanism that is timeless and universal. The divine fire, like unconditional love, is possible for all to receive.

We also believe that the kind of illumination or peak experience that the divine fire brings has been accelerating in recent years. This may be due to a time of great transition that seems to be fast approaching. Our entire species may be standing on the precipice of a great leap forward in its physical and spiritual evolution.

The increased number of illumination experiences may also be due to the fact that our nonrational needs have been neglected for decades. Materialism, competition, power politics, and commercial exploitation can be endured only so long before the human soul cries out for meaningful and personal spiritual expression.

William James has observed that the Mother Sea, the fountainhead of all religions, lies in the mystical experience of the individual. All theologies, all ecclesiastical establishments are but secondary growths superimposed.

Although the Western world has never encouraged the individual mystical experience, we believe that it is becoming clear that all people are potential mystics, just as there are potential artists, poets, and musicians.

The divine fire can be sought through a process of disciplined meditation. It can also be acquired through a devoted mystical life and a continual evolving toward cosmic consciousness. In other instances, as with Saint Paul on the road to Damascus, the illumination experience can be instantaneous—a bright light that strikes one from on high and totally alters one's life.

A third method of seeking the divine fire exists for you to utilize, and that is to become an open channel of love and peace through an altered state of consciousness.

You must believe that it is possible for you to achieve such an experience. You must prepare for it by permitting yourself to become one with the flow of the meditative energy to which you are responding at this very moment.

You must not simply ask your guide if you may have an illumination experience, you must affirm that you will. Do this now. Say within your essential self:

"I will have an illumination experience."

Next affirm that you will, from this moment onward, seek to purify and to order your life—physically, emotionally, and mentally—so that you will do all that you can to make yourself a strong receiver for the divine fire. Affirm this now, say within your essential self:

"I will seek to purify and to order my life—physically, emotionally, mentally."

Do not permit yourself to set up preconditions for the experience. Do not deliberately seek a particular message or a preconceived new understanding. Begin now to cultivate a condition of contemplation, a condition of stillness, so that when you enter the silence, you will be quiet in mind, emotions, senses, and body. Such conditions will permit the divine fire to manifest within you.

When we desire to become one with the Universe, we in one sense surrender our egos. But we must always remember balance, because we will still exist on the physical plane. Remember that we can only become channels for the divine fire and that any energy that can be used for good can be subverted. We must continually be on guard to see that our channel remains clean and open, positive and well grounded.

We must become as spiritual warriors, balancing the terror of life with the wonder of life. We must keep our spiritual swords at the ready to do battle with our true enemies—cowardice, weakness, slavish dependence upon others, greed, negativity, and chaos.

Jesus taught us that the world is arbitrary rather than an illusion or a fated absolute. He told us that the materials of the world of physical reality can be subject to dramatic change by the mind. He demonstrated that by making a total commitment to a *way* or reordering reality, we can perceive the ordinary world of reality as being but *one* of an endless number of possible constructs.

You are about to change reality, to refashion it, to reshape it, to reconstruct it.

But whatever power you receive through the divine fire, it must be voluntarily surrendered and replaced by a desire to share with others and to search out new knowledge, new revelations.

Any attempt to use this power for personal, selfish, materialistic ends will only backfire. You can, of course, use the power you receive to provide for yourself and your family. You most certainly may prosper many times over as a responsible, independent entity, so long as you do not deliberately seek to harm another or to block another's spiritual evolution.

Permit the divine fire to manifest through you and it can truly be said in the most positive way that by your works shall people know you.

You will develop deep qualities of understanding.

You will show a lack of concern toward the selfish interests of the world.

You will gain a deep sense of peace and freedom.

You will achieve a deep sense of wholeness and unity with the cosmos.

You will shift your consciousness from self to other, from "I" to "thou," from "mine" to "ours."

You will find that your physical health will manifest in increased vitality and balance.

You will develop a great patience toward your mission in life and toward the irritations sometimes brought on by others.

You will be consumed with desire to fulfill universal laws directed toward cosmic harmony.

You will become totally aware that there if a higher intelligence from which you may draw power, strength, and inspiration. The divine fire may open a channel whereby this higher intelligence will become immediately accessible to you, or it may place you in direct contact with spiritual intermediaries.

You will come to know that you have within you all that is necessary to establish communion with higher intelligence and with the Universe.

You will understand that your soul is both universal and individual.

You will comprehend that we are entering a new age, another progression in our evolution as spiritual beings. The age of secrets that encouraged priesthoods, keepers of the secrets, will soon be completed. We are moving toward a state of mystical consciousness wherein every aware human will be his or her own priest/priestess.

In the Native American medicine tradition the dogma of tribal rituals is secondary to the guidance one receives from personal visions. It is through the seeking of these visions that one becomes his or her own priest/priestess, shaman, or guru.

In the medicine tradition the vision quest is more than a

goal received. It marks the beginning of a lifelong search for wisdom and knowledge.

So it is that the illumination that comes with the divine fire marks, not a spiritual goal attained, but the beginning of a contact with a higher intelligence that will guide one throughout one's lifelong quest. The receiving of the divine fire will bring about freedom from dogma, liberation from spiritual prejudices, and the insight to become one's own priest/priestess, one's own shaman, one's own guru.

Now, affirm again from the depth of your essential self:

"I will have an illumination experience. I will seek to purify and to order my life—physically, emotionally, mentally."

At this time, quiet your mind, quiet your emotions, quiet your senses, quiet your body.

Place yourself in a deep altered state of consciousness by using one of the relaxation methods we have previously described in the book. As we have advised in other instances, you may ask a trusted friend or family member to read the following suggestions to you in a slow, thoughtful manner; or you may prerecord the suggestions in your own voice so that you may serve as your own guide. It is also possible, of course, for you to place yourself in as deep a level of relaxation as you are able to reach, then contemplate each of the thought explorations we have provided.

You will now invite the divine fire to enter your psyche and enable you to become your own guru, your own instrument of balance, love, peace, strength, and inspiration.

You know that you have within you the ability to receive a spark of the divine fire.

You know that you have the ability to be elevated to higher realms of consciousness and spiritual communion.

You know that you have the ability to become one with the Source of all that is.

You know that you have the authority to tap into the eternal transmission of universal truths from which you may draw power and strength.

You know that you have the ability to evolve as a spiritual being.

You know that you have the ability to progress out of your old, physical limitations and to rise to a higher realm.

Visualize yourself now as the kind of spiritual seeker with whom you most identify. You have this ability. You have the ability to see yourself as a monk of the European, Mideastern, Indian, or Oriental traditions.

You have the ability to see yourself as a nun, priestess, oracle, or cosmic channel.

You have the ability to see yourself as a disciplined traditional Native American on a vision quest.

You have the ability to see yourself as a druid, a wiccan, a practitioner of true magic.

Perhaps you may wish to see yourself as an enlightened alchemist, traveling through time and space.

Whatever the image you prefer, visualize yourself as that kind of spiritual seeker.

Focus your thoughts now on your performance of some mundane, monotonous physical task. Visualize yourself performing some exercise or some bit of work in a regular and measured manner.

Perhaps you are hoeing in a garden, lifting a hoe, sinking it into the ground, bending, straightening, over and over, bending, straightening, over and over...

Perhaps you are seeing yourself on your vision quest deliberately performing a task that will deplete the physical self with monotonous movements. Perhaps you have found a small clearing in the forest that has a number of rocks of various sizes at one end of the nearly barren area.

Pick up one of the rocks and carry it to the opposite side of the clearing. See yourself carrying the rock. See yourself placing the rock down on the ground and turning around to get another rock. See yourself picking up a new rock, carrying it slowly to the other side of the clearing...over...and over...and over again.

Whatever task you are seeing, know and understand

that you are doing it for the sole purpose of depleting the physical self with monotonous exercise...that you are distracting the conscious mind with dull activity...that you are doing this to free the essential self within you so that it can soar free of the physical body.

And now your body is very, very tired. It feels very heavy. It feels very dull. You have no aching muscles or sore tendons; but you are very, very tired. Your physical body is exhausted. You lie down on a blanket to rest...to rest...to relax...

Slowly you become aware of a presence.

Someone has approached you and has come to stand next to you.

Wherever you see yourself now—a forest clearing, a humble cell in a monastery or convent, a temple garden, a high mountain plateau—you are aware that someone stands near you as you rest.

As you look up at the figure, you see that it is a most impressive individual. It is a man who is looking at you with warmth and compassionate interest.

And now you notice that he has been joined by a woman who is equally impressive, almost majestic in appearance. She smiles at you, and you feel somehow as if she stands before you enveloped in the mother vibration.

Before you can open your mouth to speak the man and the woman fade from your sight. They simply disappear.

And now you realize that they were spirits, that they came to you from the spirit world to demonstrate to you that in many ways, on many levels, you have a subtle yet intense partnership with the world of spirits. The spirit man and spirit woman have given you a visual sign of the reality of this oneness with all spiritual forms of life.

You have but a moment to ponder the significance of the spirit visitation when you become aware of two globes of bluish white light moving toward you. You are not afraid, for you sense a great spiritual presence approaching you.

As you watch in reverential expectation, the first globe

of bluish white light begins to assume human form.

As the light swirls and becomes solid, you behold before you a man or a woman whom you regard as a holy person, a saint, a master, an illumined one. This figure, so beloved to you, gestures to your left side. As you turn, you are astonished to see a marvelous linkup of other holy figures from all times, from all places, from all cultures. You see that these personages form a beautiful spiritual chain, from prehistory to the present and without doubt, the future.

The holy one smiles benevolently, then bends over you and touches your shoulder. Then gently the holy one's forefinger lightly touches first your eyes, then your ears, then your mouth. You know within that this touching symbolizes that you are about to see and to hear a wondrous revelation, which, consequently, you must share with others.

As the holy figure begins to fade from your perception, the second globe of bluish white light begins to materialize into human form.

The entity that forms before you now may be very familiar to you. You may very likely have seen this entity in your dreams. You may even have seen this entity materialize before you on previous occasions. You may have been aware of this entity since your earliest memories, for standing before you now is your guide.

See the love in those eyes. Feel the love emanating toward you from your guide. This is one who has always loved you just as you are. This is one who has always totally accepted you just as you are. This is one who, with unconditional love, is concerned completely with your spiritual evolution.

You feel totally relaxed, at peace, at one with your guide. And you feel totally loved.

Your guide's mouth is opening. Listen. Listen to the sound that issues forth. You hear it clearly and you understand it.

It may be a personal sound—a mantra. It may be a series

of notes and words—your own personal song. It may be your guide's name.

Whatever the sound is, you hear it clearly and distinctly. And you have the inner awareness that whenever you repeat this sound—this mantra, this song, this name—you will be able to achieve instant oneness with your guide.

Your guide is now showing you something important. Your guide's hands are holding something for you to see.

It is an object you can clearly identify that will serve as a symbol that you are about to receive a meaningful and important teaching in your dreams.

Whenever you see this symbol in your dreams, you will understand that an important and significant teaching will follow.

The symbol fades from your sight, but you will remember it.

You are fascinated by what your guide now holds before you.

In your guide's hands is a tiny flame, a flame such as one might see on a match or a candle. The flame flickers and dances. You cannot take your eyes from it.

The flame seems to capture all of your attention and to pull you toward it. It is as if your very spirit is being pulled from your body and drawn toward the flame.

The flame is becoming brighter—brighter and larger. You cannot take your eyes from this strange, compelling flame. You can no longer see your guide. You can see only the flame. You are no longer aware of anything other than the flame. It is growing larger, larger and brighter, brighter and larger. It is as if there is nothing else in the entire Universe but the flame—the flame and *you*.

You know now that this is the divine fire. You know now that this flame has appeared to bring you illumination. You know that it is not really a fire, not really a flame, but a divine and holy energy, the same energy that is interwoven with all of life, the same energy that interacts with all of life.

This energy now swirls around you, lightly tingling the

body whenever it touches you. It is not at all an unpleasant sensation. It is, in fact, soothing, yet strangely exhilarating at the same time.

The energy now caresses your body gently, lovingly.

You are aware of your body becoming cleansed, purified, healed of any ills, pains, and tensions:

You know that from this moment onward your physical health is going to be superb, better than it has ever been.

You know that from this moment on, your physical energy is going to be increased.

You know that your friends and your family will be commenting about your golden glow of health and vitality.

The energy of the divine fire now enters your body. It is now becoming one with you. It is becoming one with your cleansed and purified body. It is becoming one with your expectant spirit.

In a great rush of color and light you now find yourself elevated in spirit. You have moved to a higher vibrational level. You have moved to a dimension where nonlinear time, cyclical time, flows around you. From your previous limited perspective of Earth-time, linear time, you are aware that you now exist in a timeless realm.

Stretching before you is something that appears to be a gigantic tapestry, a tapestry that has been woven of multicolored living lights, lights that are pulsating, throbbing with life. The lights have blended together, become one yet they somehow remain separate. All colors and shadings of colors imaginable are stretched out before you.

The energy of the divine fire touches your inner self and you are aware that you are becoming one with the great tapestry of life. In a marvelous moving, pulsating thrust of beautiful lights and living energy, your very essence feels a unity with all living things.

See before you an animal, any animal.
Become one with its essence.
Become one with its level of awareness.

Be that animal.
Be that level of energy expression.
See before you a bird, any bird.
Become one with its essence.
Become one with its level of awareness.
Be that bird.
Be that level of energy expression.
See before you a creature of the waters, any creature.
Become one with its essence.
Become one with its level of awareness.
Be that marine creature.
Be that level of energy expression.
See before you an insect, any insect, crawling or flying.
Become one with its essence.
Become one with its level of awareness.
Be that insect.
Be that level of energy expression.
See before you a plant, any flower, tree, grass, or shrub.
Become one with its essence.
Become one with its level of awareness.
Be that plant.
Be that level of energy expression.

Know now that you are one with the unity of all plant and animal essence. Know now that you forever bear responsibility to all plant and animal life. You are one with all things that walk on two legs or four, with all things that fly, with all things that crawl, with all things that grow in the soil or sustain themselves in the waters.

See before you now a person, man or woman, that you find unattractive, perhaps even ugly.
Become one with this person's essence.
Become one with this person's level of awareness.
Be that person.
Be that level of energy expression.
See before you a child, boy or girl.

Become one with this child's essence.
Become one with this child's level of awareness.
Be that child.
Be that level of energy expression.
See before you now a very old man or woman, perhaps someone confined to a bed or wheelchair.
Become one with that old person's essence.
Become one with that old person's level of awareness.
Be that old person.
Be that level of energy expression.

Know now that it is never yours to judge another expression of humankind. Know now that you have a common brotherhood and sisterhood with all of humankind. Remember always that you must do unto your brothers and sisters as you would have them do to you. Remember always that the great error is to prevent in any way another's spiritual evolution.

At this eternal second in the energy of the eternal now, at this vibrational level of oneness with all living things, at this frequency of awareness of unity with one cosmos, the divine fire is permitting you to receive a great teaching vision of something about which you need to know for your good and your gaining. Receive this great vision—now! (Pause here for approximately three minutes to receive impressions.)

You will awaken at the count of five, filled with memories of your great vision. When you awaken you will feel morally elevated; you will feel intellectually illuminated; you will know that your essence is immortal; you will no longer fear death; you will no longer experience guilt or a sense of sin; you will feel filled with great charm and personal magnetism; you will feel better and healthier than ever before in your life; you will feel a great sense of unity with all living things.

One...two...three...four...five...awaken!

20

A Final Reminder

You should consider this book to be your cosmic tool kit in building your greater awareness of self, of reality, and of your relationship to the Universe. Now that you have read our book and had an opportunity to experience many of the techniques contained within these pages, it is our sincere hope that you have come to a number of realizations.

You can now unlock previously hidden powers of your mind and transform your life with guided meditation.

You can now contact the light within you and use it, understand it, and explore it.

You can now become free of the physical limitations of time and space, visit other worlds, other Universes, and contact higher intelligences on many levels of reality.

You can now find your own path to the Source.

The operative word in each of the above affirmations is *you*. As with any set of tools, the manipulator of those implements must bring a certain amount of skill, desire, and commitment to the task if it is to be successful.

We have tried to be as helpful as we could in providing you with the tools you may use in your independent quest, but we cannot build your path for you. You must maintain an attitude of openness and receptivity to the experiences we describe and to the techniques we share in this book.

No one can lead you into an altered state of consciousness or to a higher level of awareness if you do not wish it. If you have read these chapters with the mental challenge, "I'll bet these techniques won't work for me," you have won the bet.

No one in the world can give you awareness but you yourself. What we have attempted to do is to guide you carefully, lovingly through a number of significant experiences that will help to awaken the awareness within you. The formula is really very simple: If you wish to enter an altered state and explore beyond yourself, you can. If you block awareness or resist it, you will not be other than you were.

You will always be most successful in working with this book if you set all negativity aside from you when you sit or lie down in a quiet place to enter the total experience of raising your consciousness. This book should be read with a wonderful sense of expectancy for what you may receive during your inner voyage of discovery.

Several times during the course of the text we have mentioned that we share these techniques and meditations with you in an attitude of unconditional love. We have also emphasized the point that we do not seek to alter anyone's belief structure. We wish only to be light bearers shining a light so that you will be able to see your own path more clearly.

In conclusion, though, we would like to share with you our own belief structure.

We believe that the essence of all religions lies in the mystical experience of the individual, and that all theologies and all dogmas are but secondary growths superimposed on this basic experience.

There is a Supreme Being, timeless and universal, to whom all men and all women may reach out to receive strength.

Humankind is part of a larger community of intelligences, a complex heirarchy of powers and principalities, a potentially richer kingdom of interrelated species—both physical and nonphysical. Among these intelligences are certain multidimensional beings who care about us and our spiritual evolution.

Humankind's one truly essential factor is its spirituality. The artificial worlds to which humankind has given the designation of sciences are no truer than dreams, visions, and inspirations. The quest for absolute proof or objective truth may always be meaningless and unattainable when it seeks to define or to limit humankind's soul.

The soul is eternal, evolving higher and higher in spiritual vibrations, seeking to return to the Source from whence it came. We accept the karmic laws of balance and compensation and the concept that the soul may live many lifetimes in order to gain learning experiences for its good and its evolution to the Source.

We believe that the technological plays a far smaller role in the lives of nations than the spiritual, for the essence of humankind is its intellect and its soul. The only lasting truths are soul, imagination, and inspiration. Machines, associations, political parties, and trade balances are but transitory realities that must ultimately wither, decay, and come to nothing.

Each man and each woman, in moments of quiet meditation, may learn to enter the silence, enrich the soul, and achieve a spiritual linkup with the blessed harmony that governs the Universe.

It is our sincere desire that this book will enable you to achieve a higher state of awareness. We pray that the techniques we have shared with you will permit you to undergo a series of experiences that will truly help you to make more complete sense out of your life than you have ever before been able to comprehend. We ask for your continued enlightenment as you live your life as a spiritual quest that will return your energy to the Source.

There are many fine New Age musicians who produce ethereal sounds that will make beautiful background music for your inward journeys. We use primarily the creations of Steven Halpern in our own cassettes and seminars.

Those who wish information regarding our regressive, meditative, and inspirational cassette recordings may write to us through our publisher. Please enclose a stamped, self-addressed envelope.

Brad Steiger
c/o Schiffer Publishing Co.
1469 Morstein Road
West Chester, Pennsylvania 19380

Discover Your Past Lives

Brad Steiger is an internationally known psychic researcher and the author of more than one hundred books in the metaphysical, psychic and inspirational fields. He also has written scripts for several motion pictures and documentaries, and is a regular contributor to numerous magazines and newspapers. In 1987, he was selected for the International Hypnosis Hall of Fame. Mr. Steiger lives in Arizona.

Frances Pascal Steiger is one of the world's leading mystics. She is also a teacher, author, researcher and lecturer. She appears frequently on radio and television shows, is a regular contributor to national and international magazines, and has written several books in the inspirational and human potential fields. The founder and president of the *Star People Foundation*, Ms. Steiger is dedicated to enlightening the world and improving life on earth.

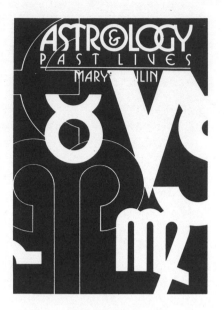

ASTROLOGY & PAST LIVES

Mary Devlin

This unique and original book is the first to examine birth charts for previous incarnations. Devlin shows you how to interpret past-life charts and compare them to your present one. By studying astrological patterns that repeat in chart after chart, lifetime after lifetime, you'll discover that many of your current experiences, relationships and attitudes are rooted in past existences.

Astrology & Past Lives is the result of ten years of research and hundreds of case studies. More than sixty charts and corresponding case histories—of both famous and ordinary people, past and present—are included as examples.

0-914918-71-0
304 pages, 6½" x 9¼", paper

$18.95

ASTRAL PROJECTION

Brad Steiger

Parapsychological researchers have established that one of every one hundred persons has experienced out-of-body projection (OBE). These experiences are not limited to any single type of person, but rather they cross all typical boundaries.

In *Astral Projection*, Brad Steiger, investigates the phenomenon of OBE and correlates those events into broad categories for analysis and explanation. In his clear and non-sensational style, Steiger relates how these spontaneous experiences occur and when they are likely to re-occur. In addition to the standard and well-documented categories of spontaneous astral projection at times of stress, sleep, death and near-death, Steiger devotes considerable time to the growing evidence for conscious out-of-body experiences, where the subject deliberately seeks to cast his or her spirit out of the physical shell.

Along with his study of astral projection, Steiger sets guidelines for astral travellers, tells them the dangers they may face and how this type of psychic experience might be used for medical diagnosis, therapy and self-knowledge.

Author Brad Steiger is your guide to controlling astral projection and using it for your own benefit.

ISBN 0-914918-36-2
234 pages, 6½" x 9¼", paper

$12.95

KAHUNA MAGIC

Brad Steiger

Based on the life work of Max Freedom Long, *Kahuna Magic* lays open the secrets of the Kahuna, the ancient Hawaiian priests. Long used the secrets of the Hawaiian language to unlock the secrets of this powerful and mystical discipline.

Long was a much-respected psychic researcher. His student Brad Steiger chronicles Long's adventures on the way to understanding the magic of the Kahuna. By following Long's trek, the reader will learn how the Kahunas used their magic for both the benefit of their friends and the destruction of their enemies.

Central to the Huna beliefs was the thesis that each person has three selves. The Low Self is the emotive spirit, dealing in basic wants and needs. The Middle Self is the self operating at the everyday level. The High Self is the spiritual being that is in contact with every other High Self.

The subject matter of *Kahuna Magic* is contemporary and compelling. The book incorporates many of the concepts and concerns of the modern Western psychological tradition of Jung and Freud while bringing in subjects as diverse as Eastern philosophies and yoga in a manner that will help the readers understand themselves and those around them.

ISBN 0-914918-34-6
127 pages, 6½″ × 9¼″, paper

$10.95